Doing a Dam Better

The Lao People's Democratic Republic and the Story of Nam Theun 2

Dear Nadine and Bob,

Thank you so much for all your support and encouragement over many years on this and other projects. I hope you enjoy reading the book.

Lots of love

Doing a Dam Better

The Lao People's Democratic Republic and the Story of Nam Theun 2

Ian C. Porter and Jayasankar Shivakumar

Editors

ISBN: 978-0-8213-6985-2
eISBN: 978-0-8213-6986-9
DOI: 10.1596/978-0-8213-6985-2

Library of Congress Cataloging-in-Publication Data
Doing a dam better : the Lao People's Democratic Republic and the story of Nam Theun 2 /
   edited by Ian C. Porter and Jayasankar Shivakumar.
      p. cm.
   Includes bibliographical references and index.
   ISBN 978-0-8213-6985-2 — ISBN 978-0-8213-6986-9 (electronic)
   1. Hydroelectric power plants—Laos. 2. Economic development projects—
Laos. I. Porter, Ian C. II. Shivakumar, Jayasankar, 1938– III. World Bank.
   TK1513.L28D65 2010
   333.91'409594--dc22
                                                          2009052160

Cover photographs: Elephant in Nakai Plateau-watershed area, Lao PDR by Didier Goetzinger,
© NTPC; forest in Lao PDR by Uwe Bauch, © istockphoto.com/uba-foto; all others
© The World Bank

Images from the Nam Theun 2 Project (between pp. 126 and 127): © The World Bank

Cover design: Critical Stages

Dedication and Recognition

This book is dedicated to the Lao people, who have displayed remarkable patience and understanding over the years of preparation of the Nam Theun 2 project.

Many individuals around the globe worked tirelessly to make the NT2 project happen and their contributions merit special recognition.

Contents

Foreword

The Nam Theun 2 (NT2) Hydroelectric Project emerged from a special confluence of circumstances. The Government of the Lao People's Democratic
Republic (PDR) saw that the project could provide an opportunity to make
great strides toward its development goals to help lift its people out of poverty.
The developers saw an occasion to demonstrate that a large, complex infrastructure project could be undertaken successfully in a small, poor country despite the enormousness of the obstacles presented. And the World Bank
Group and other development partners endeavored to meet the challenge of
supporting the country's and the developers' efforts through engagement on a
set of related interventions—including infrastructure development, support
for a range of environmental and social programs and policies, and strengthening of public financial management—to ensure that the project was well
prepared and embedded in a strong national development strategy.

To turn the opportunities into achievements, enormous effort has been put
forth over many years by all parties engaged. From the World Bank Group
perspective, several elements have been key to the achievements to date. The
Government of Lao PDR considers the project a national priority and an integral element of its long-term development vision—and has sustained the
commitment needed to undertake the preparatory work and longer-term reforms necessary to pave the way for the project to achieve the desired development objectives. The developers have also been committed to making the
project a success for Lao PDR by ensuring that the obligations, project standards, and environmental and social safeguards are met. Support for the
broader NT2 program (including related interventions) has enabled a more
holistic, cross-sectoral approach to sustainable infrastructure development,
which has broadened the impact of the project. Over the years, the dialogue
on NT2 and related matters has facilitated a deepening of relationships between the Government and the World Bank (as well as other involved donors
and the developers). Furthermore, strong partnerships have been forged and

maintained among a large number of international financial institutions involved in the project, providing a cohesive and complementary package of support for Lao PDR's efforts and the project financing. Finally, stakeholder participation in this project has been notable, as has been the availability of public information. Local consultations and international workshops have been undertaken to an unprecedented degree for Lao PDR, and the availability of public information has been considerable, providing a level of transparency that has enabled all interested parties to readily track project progress.

NT2 is now in commercial operation and contributing significant revenues to Government. The East Asia and Pacific Region of the World Bank, under my stewardship, will continue to be closely involved with the project, particularly in regard to safeguards and revenue management issues. I must also recognize the remarkable contribution made by my predecessor, Jemal-ud-din Kassum, to the oversight needed to bring this transformational project to fruition.

As with any complex, large undertaking, there are important lessons to be learned—and NT2 is no exception. This book gathers a body of thoughts and findings, from a broad range of experience, expertise, and perspective of persons, mobilized to this end by the editors, who themselves are World Bank alumni with a long and close association with the project. Because of the special circumstances surrounding NT2, not all of the experiences and lessons will be relevant for other countries and other hydropower projects. But I am confident that the story of NT2 described in this publication will help spur further efforts by the community of development practitioners to do dams even better in the future.

James W. Adams
Vice President
East Asia and Pacific Region
The World Bank

November 2010

Preface

The purpose of this book is to share with development practitioners the experiences gained and lessons learned during the preparation of the $1.45 billion Nam Theun 2 (NT2) hydroelectric power project in the Lao People's Democratic Republic. This book focuses on the project preparation exercise. It also provides a brief assessment of implementation experience so far, a subject that deserves more thorough treatment after some more years of commercial operations.

The book is a reflection of a World Bank–led exercise to extract and disseminate lessons learned during project preparation. To deepen the value of that exercise, the authors have also gained fresh perspectives and insights through exchanges of views with a broad range of project participants. The resulting candid and varied collection of perspectives is purposefully retained, unfettered by attempts to promote consistency among the views of the different authors. And, as such, the opinions expressed in this book do not represent the official views of the World Bank Group.

Maximizing the development impact of a hydroelectric dam is a journey, not a destination. As the journey continues, more knowledge will be gained, more lessons will be learned and applied, and new solutions will be defined and shaped to address the evolving challenges of "doing a dam better." It is hoped that the World Bank Group will continue to facilitate the exchange of views with its partners and other stakeholders on the experiences gained, not only through project preparation but also during project implementation.

We are deeply grateful to a large number of development practitioners—too many to name individually—who graciously shared their time and knowledge. At the institutional level, we owe a deep debt of gratitude to the Government of Lao PDR; the Royal Thai Government; the World Bank's financial partners, both public and private, including the international financial institutions supporting the project; the Nam Theun 2 Power Company (NTPC); and a number of civil society organizations. We are also grateful to the contributions of many World Bank staff and consultants. We especially want to recognize the chapter authors: Nazir Ahmad, Rosa Alonso i Terme, Mara T. Baranson, Ram Chopra, Patchamuthu Illangovan, Homi Kharas, Mark Segal, Teresa Serra, Peter Stephens, and the Duke Center for International Development. This book would not have been possible without their expertise, insights, and deep understanding of the development process.

We would also like to thank James D. Wolfensohn, Shengman Zhang, Jemal-ud-din Kassum, Ngozi Okonjo-Iweala, Callisto Madavo, Jean-Michel Severino, and Rajat Nag for providing the leadership needed at the World Bank and its development partners to help bring NT2 to fruition. Furthermore, considerable appreciation is extended to the external, independent advisory panels such as the Environmental and Social Panel of Experts, the International Advisory Group, and the Dam Safety Review Panel for their guidance over the years. Finally, we would like to thank our developmental editors, Mark Feige and Mara T. Baranson, the World Bank Office of the Publisher's Patricia Katayama and Aziz Gökdemir, and Barbara Karni for their advice and support.

Ian C. Porter
Jayasankar Shivakumar

About the Editors and Contributors

IAN PORTER has more than 30 years' international development experience. During his career at the World Bank, he served as Country Director for South East Asia when Nam Theun 2 was undertaken. He was also Manager of Policy Support for the Board of Directors, Division Chief for Population and Human Resources in West Africa, and Resident Representative for Tanzania. Earlier in his career, he worked on economic and sectoral reform issues in China, Thailand, and Vietnam. Before joining the World Bank, he worked for the government of Malawi as an Overseas Development Institute Fellow. He holds an M.A. in development economics from Sussex University.

JAYASANKAR SHIVAKUMAR served the World Bank in staff, managerial, and consultant positions for more than three decades, working mainly on East Asian and East African countries. He has been associated with the Lao PDR Nam Theun 2 project in various managerial and advisory capacities since 1994. He was based in Bangkok as the World Bank's Country Director for Thailand during that country's period of economic crisis. Since his retirement, in 2001, he has worked as a consultant to the World Bank on development activities in East and South Asia. He held positions in the Indian Administrative Service from 1961 to 1977. He holds an M.Sc in physics from Delhi University and an MPA from Harvard University.

About the Contributors

NAZIR AHMAD is the president of Giving Works Inc., a strategy consultancy firm providing advice to premier public service institutions, including the World Bank, UNICEF, and the Soros Foundation. Before launching Giving

Works, in 2002, he was a partner and practice leader at Strategic Decisions Group, where he advised global corporations on leadership, business innovation, strategic marketing, business alliances, and capacity building. He holds an M.A. in international development economics and an MBA from Stanford University.

ROSA ALONSO I TERME is a senior public sector specialist in the Poverty Reduction and Economic Management Unit of the East Asia and Pacific region of the World Bank. She has served as an economist at the International Monetary Fund, a senior economist at the World Bank Institute, and a regional adviser for poverty reduction strategies in the East Asia and Pacific region of the World Bank. She has also been a visiting professor at the University of Barcelona, Georgetown University, Tel Aviv University, and Bethlehem University. She holds an English philology degree and a law degree from the University of Barcelona and an M.A. and Ph.D. in international economics and European studies from the School of Advanced International Studies of Johns Hopkins University.

MARA T. BARANSON is a consultant to the World Bank, where she has worked on the Nam Theun 2 hydroelectric project since 2001. Before coming to the World Bank, she spent more than a decade at JPMorgan. Her consulting focus is on complex projects in developing countries. She holds an M.A. in international business studies from the University of South Carolina.

RAM CHOPRA held various management positions at the World Bank, including Country Director for the Middle East Department and Global Director for Project Finance and Co-financing, where he was responsible for the World Bank's dealings with multilateral and bilateral aid agencies and the Bank's Guarantee Program. After leaving the World Bank, he served as a managing director of Chase Bank, where he dealt with project finance and agency co-financing. He was a Rhodes Scholar at Oxford University, where he completed a postgraduate degree in economics.

PATCHAMUTHU ILLANGOVAN was the World Bank's Country Manager for Lao PDR between 2005 and 2010. Prior to that he was Sector Coordinator for Environment and Social Development for the South East Asia Country Management Unit, Lead Environment Specialist for the East Asia and Pacific region, and Senior Environment Specialist for the South Asia and the East Asia and Pacific regions. In this capacity, he led several technical teams and tasks in environmental institutions, water resources management, and urban environmental management. Before joining the World Bank in 1993, he worked with both the public and the private sectors in his native Sri Lanka in a number of technical and managerial roles. He has been associated with the Nam Theun 2 Project since 2002, when he became the Team Leader for the project's Environment and Social Program. He holds a Master of Engineering Degree in environmental technology and management from the Asian Institute of Technology, Bangkok, Thailand.

HOMI KHARAS is a senior fellow at the Wolfensohn Center for Development at the Brookings Institution, in Washington, DC. While at the World Bank, he served as Chief Economist and Director of the East Asia and Pacific region. His research interests now focus on global trends, East Asian growth and development, and international aid for the poorest countries. He holds a Ph.D. in economics from Harvard University.

MARK SEGAL is a consultant in energy economics, specializing in the economic appraisal of major hydro, thermal, and transmission investments. He has served as principal economist in the Electric Power Department of the International Finance Corporation, senior economist in the Industry and Energy practice of the World Bank's West Africa Operations Department, and chief economist of the National Energy Board of Canada. He holds an M.A. in economics from McGill University.

TERESA SERRA is a consultant with more than 30 years of experience in environmental and social issues in developing countries. During her 15-year tenure at the World Bank, she served as Director of the Environment and Social Development Department of the East Asia and Pacific region and as Sector Manager for Environment in Latin America and the Caribbean. She was actively involved in many urban, transport, energy, mining, and environment projects. Before joining the World Bank, she established and headed the Environment Department at Eletrobras, at the time Brazil's coordinating agency for power system planning, financing, and operation. She holds master's degrees in urban and regional planning and in economics from the University of California, Berkeley.

PETER STEPHENS worked as a journalist for 20 years, from 1974 to 1993, covering political and economic affairs, labor relations, and international affairs. He was appointed Washington Correspondent for the Australian newspaper *The Age* in 1989, with oversight of coverage across the Western Hemisphere, as well as superpower summits involving the United States and the Soviet Union. He joined the World Bank as a communications officer in the East Asia and Pacific region vice-presidency in 1993 and subsequently was appointed to oversee the Bank's Singapore Office as well as manage a regional communications team spanning 12 countries. He was a member of the East Asia and Pacific region management team. In 2008, he was reassigned to Washington, DC, as Director of Operational Communications at the World Bank, a position he currently holds.

THE DUKE CENTER FOR INTERNATIONAL DEVELOPMENT (DCID) at the Sanford School of Public Policy, Duke University, is dedicated to "strengthening capacity for international development through interdisciplinary approaches to knowledge and innovations in practice, research, professional advice, midcareer training, and postgraduate education." The DCID team that assisted the World Bank in identifying the cross-cutting operational lessons from the Nam Theun 2 experience was led by the late Dennis Rondinelli and Gary M. Nelson. DENNIS RONDINELLI was a senior research scholar in public policy studies at Duke University. He holds a Ph.D. in urban and regional planning, public administration, and managerial economics from Cornell University. GARY M. NELSON is a senior fellow with the Center for Global Initiatives at the University of North Carolina at Chapel Hill. He holds a Ph.D. in social welfare from the University of California, Berkeley. Team members included Jonathan Abels, Rosemary Fernholz, Francis Lethem, and Natalia Mirovitskaya. JONATHAN ABELS is the executive director of DCID. He holds an M.A. in history from Duke University. ROSEMARY FERNHOLZ is a senior research scholar and lecturing fellow in public policy at Duke University. She holds a Ph.D. in political economy and government from Harvard University. FRANCIS LETHEM is the director of DCID and professor of the practice of public policy studies at Duke University. He holds a Ph.D. in economics from University of Neuchâtel (Switzerland). NATALIA MIROVITSKAYA is a senior research scholar and lecturing fellow in public policy at Duke University. She holds a Ph.D. in economics from the Russian Academy of Science.

Abbreviations

ADB	Asian Development Bank
AFD	Agence Française du Développement
AFTA	ASEAN Free Trade Agreement
ASEAN	Association of Southeast Asian Nations
CCGT	combined-cycle gas turbines
COFACE	Compagnie Française d'Assurance pour le Commerce Extérieur (French Export Credit Agency)
CPIA	Country Policy and Institutional Assessment
DPL	Development Policy Loan
EdF	Electricité de France
EDFI	Electricité de France International
EGAT	Electricity Generating Authority of Thailand
EGCO	Electricity Generating Public Company of Thailand
EIB	European Investment Bank
EIRR	expected internal rate of return
EKN	Exportkreditnamnden (Swedish Export Credit Agency)
EMDP	Ethnic Minorities Development Plan
FMAC	Financial Management and Adjustment Credit
FMCBC	Financial Management Capacity Building Credit
GDP	gross domestic product
GIEK	Guarantee Institute for Export Credits (Norway)
GNI	gross national income
IAG	International Advisory Group (of the World Bank)
IDA	International Development Association
IMF	International Monetary Fund
ITD	Italian Thai Development Public Company
IUCN	International Union for Conservation of Nature
Lao PDR	Lao People's Democratic Republic
MDG	Millennium Development Goal

MIGA	Multilateral Investment and Guarantee Agency
MRC	Mekong River Commission
NGO	nongovernmental organization
NGPES	National Growth and Poverty Eradication Strategy
NIB	Nordic Investment Bank
NNT-NPA	Nakai-Nam Theun National Protected Area
NSEDP	National Socio-Economic Development Plan
NT2	Nam Theun 2
NTEC	Nam Theun 2 Electricity Consortium
NTPC	Nam Theun 2 Power Company
NTSEP	Nam Theun 2 Social and Environment Project
OCR	Ordinary Capital Resources
OP	Operational Policy
PEMSP/PFMSP	Public Expenditure/Financial Management Strengthening Program
PRG	political risk guarantee
PRSC	Poverty Reduction Support Credit
PRSO	Poverty Reduction Support Operation
PRSP	Poverty Reduction Strategy Paper
SDP	Social Development Plan
WCD	World Commission on Dams
WMPA	Watershed Management and Protection Authority

All dollar figures are U.S. dollars.

CHAPTER 1

Overview

Ian Porter and Jayasankar Shivakumar

Preparation of the $1.45 billion[1] Nam Theun 2 (NT2) project in the Lao People's Democratic Republic (Lao PDR) represented an important milestone for the government, the developers, international partners, and other stakeholders. The story of its preparation and implementation is an important one, because it provides valuable insights and lessons that can be applied in future projects of similar size, scope, and complexity.

Projects this size are always complex. NT2 was particularly complicated, however, because it was prepared during the challenging times that included the dam debate of the 1990s, which culminated in the World Commission on Dams, the Asian financial crisis of 1997, the strengthening of environmental and social safeguard policies and practices at the World Bank and other financial institutions, and the greater scrutiny of governance arrangements for the transparent use of natural resource rents by countries. This book covers those times and focuses on the widely differing perspectives of NT2's diverse stakeholders, the unique political economy of Lao PDR, the heated international debate on dams, the rapidly changing state of the art regarding poverty and safeguard interventions, the shifting signals within the World Bank, and the collective efforts of many different partners and stakeholders to ensure that NT2 met the high and appropriate standards.

NT2 has had a major impact on the government of Lao PDR, the hydropower industry, the World Bank and other financial institutions, civil society groups, and others closely following hydropower development. It is important for five main reasons:

- It is a cornerstone of the growth and poverty reduction strategy of a poor country that is rich in natural resources.

1

- It reflects a shift in the mindset of the political leadership and government of Lao PDR, which undertook bold reforms and at the same time signaled the desire to engage more closely with the global community and to open up space for dialogue at home.
- It represents the first time a truly diverse set of large investors from all over the world participated in a project in Lao PDR.
- It provides strong evidence of the World Bank's reengagement in the hydropower sector.
- It demonstrates that hydropower projects can be designed and implemented to deliver sustainable outcomes through state-of-the-art environmental and social practices and strengthened public financial management systems, but this takes a long time.

Background of the NT2 Project

More than three decades ago, what is now the Secretariat of the Mekong River Commission developed an indicative plan for developing hydropower in the Mekong basin.[2] The plan included a long list of promising hydropower projects, including three large sites in the lower Mekong basin along the Nam Theun River. Following additional feasibility studies, the middle site, NT2, emerged as the best option for development. In 1993 an exclusive mandate was granted to begin development of NT2 as a private sector investment project (in which the government would hold a 25 percent equity share), primarily for the export of power to Thailand.

NT2 is located in the central part of Lao PDR, with a geographic footprint that touches three provinces (primarily Khammouane Province, with some features located in Bolikhamxay and Savannaket provinces). The site's unique topography is extremely favorable to the production of hydropower. The site is also located near the watershed for the river—the Nakai Nam Theun National Protected Area, a 4,013-square-kilometer area with world-class biodiversity surrounding the source of the river. (See NT2 map, inside front cover.)

NT2 is a trans-basin-diversion project affecting two rivers (figure 1.1; box 1.1). Water from the Nam Theun River is dammed to form a reservoir on the Nakai plateau; a small flow continues into the Nam Theun River downstream of the dam. Most of the water from the reservoir travels through an intake structure into a headrace tunnel and then to a vertical pressure shaft that goes down through the rock escarpment—dropping an average of about 348 meters in elevation from the reservoir—through a horizontal pressure

Figure 1.1 Schematic of the Nam Theun 2 Project

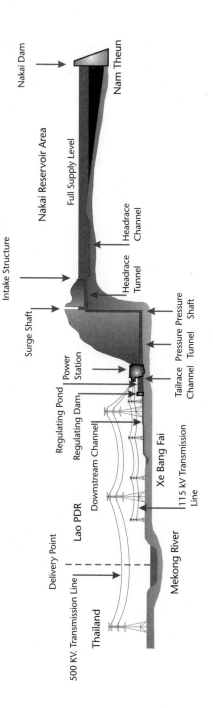

Source: Data provided by Nam Theun 2 Power Company (www.namtheun2.com).
Note: kV = kilovolt.

Box 1.1
Features of the NT2 Project

NT2 is on the Nam Theun River, a tributary of the Mekong. Key features of the project include the following:

- A 39-meter-high, 436-meter-long concrete gravity dam with integrated spillway
- A 450-square-kilometer reservoir and 3,530-million-cubic-meter active storage area
- A 4,039-square-kilometer catchment area
- An average net head of water of 348 meters
- A powerhouse comprising 4 x 250 MW Francis turbines (for supply of power to EGAT) and 2 x 37.5 MW Pelton turbines (for supply of power to EDL)
- A 115 kV double-circuit transmission line to Mahaxai, in Lao PDR.
- A 500 kV double-circuit transmission line to the Thai border.[a]

Source: Nam Theun 2 Power Company Web site (www.namtheun2.com).
a. In addition, a 500 kV double-circuit transmission line runs from the Thai border to Roi Et (built and funded by EGAT).

---

tunnel to reach the power station. The significant head (the change in elevation from the top to the bottom of a column of water) allows NT2 to make optimum use of the pressure of falling water, enabling the scheme to include a much lower dam than would otherwise be needed for comparable hydropower output. The water passing through the power plant exits into a tailrace channel leading to a regulating pond and regulating dam, which then directs water into a 27-kilometer-long downstream channel that flows into the Xe Bang Fai River, which eventually joins the Mekong River downstream of the Nam Theun River.

The NT2 project that was approved by the World Bank in 2005 has a development objective of generating revenues, through the environmentally and socially sustainable development of NT2's hydropower potential, that will be used to finance priority poverty reduction and environmental management programs. The project has been developed as a build-own-operate-transfer scheme, with the government granting a 25-year concession to the developers to build, own, and operate the power station, after which full ownership of the NT2 assets transfers to the government, at no cost. The project includes three main components:

- Development, construction, and operation of a 1,070 MW power plant and related facilities, which will export about 995 MW of generating capacity and electrical energy to Thailand and supply 75 MW to Electricité du Laos (EDL) for domestic consumption

- Management of the project's environmental and social impacts on the Nakai plateau, in the NT2 watershed, and in the downstream areas of the Nam Theun and Xe Bang Fai rivers
- Monitoring and evaluation designed to meet sound engineering practices, fiduciary responsibilities, and the oversight requirements of the participating financial institutions in a timely and cost-effective manner.

Lao PDR and the Case for NT2

Lao PDR is a small, landlocked, sparsely populated, and poor country. It covers an area of 236,800 square kilometers and shares borders with Cambodia, China, Myanmar, Thailand, and Vietnam, situating it in the center of the dynamic Mekong region. It has a population of about 6.0 million and had an estimated per capita income of about $740 in 2008, making it one of the poorest countries in East Asia. Lao PDR is also a country with extensive natural resources of water (used for hydroelectricity generation); tropical forests (covering 47 percent of its land area); and minerals (including copper, gold, gemstones, and gypsum).

Economic Development in Lao PDR

In the 1990s and early 2000s, Lao PDR's economy grew at an annual average rate of 6.3 percent. Per capita income rose from $270 in 1993 to $450 in 2005 (*World Development Indicators*). There was also a significant decline in the incidence of poverty, which fell from 45 percent of the population in 1992/93 to 39 percent in 1997/98 and 33 percent in 2002/03 (using the national poverty line) and from 59 percent in 1992/93 to 49 percent in 1997/98 and 44 percent in 2002/03 based on the World Bank's new $1.25-a-day 2005 purchasing power parity measure. Lao PDR has also been making progress toward meeting some of the Millennium Development Goals (MDGs), although it is off track for meeting others. The under-five mortality rate plummeted from 163 per 1,000 in 1990 to 70 per 1,000 in 2007, for example, but the prevalence of malnourished children under the age of five held constant, at 40 percent.

The generally positive economic and social progress of recent years has been encouraged by the economic reforms pursued by the government. The New Economic Mechanism (NEM) for national development introduced by the government in 1986 began the transition from a centrally planned to a market-oriented economy, while maintaining a single-party political system. Subsequent plans have endeavored to continue with the reform process. The 2004 National Growth and Poverty Eradication Strategy (NGPES) reinforced the importance of further macroeconomic measures and structural reforms while emphasizing that natural resource development, especially hydropower and mining, will be integral to the development strategy for sustaining past growth rates and achieving the MDGs.

The NGPES included an annual growth target of 7–8 percent over the next decade.[3] Continued growth of the agriculture, manufacturing, and services sectors is expected to yield growth of about 5–6 percent a year. Developing mining and hydropower—which together are projected to add 2–3 percentage points of GDP growth a year—should help Lao PDR meet the NGPES goal. But developing these sectors in a sound manner from an environmental and social as well as technical and financial perspective will be a major challenge. The country also faces other challenges as it continues to move toward a market-oriented system, including limited capacity in the central and provincial governments, lack of infrastructure, a fledgling private sector, and the limited engagement of stakeholders in the development debate.

Strategic Role of NT2 in Lao PDR

The NGPES identified the power sector as one of the potential drivers of growth. The sector serves two national priorities. First, it promotes economic and social advancement by providing a reliable, affordable, and sustainable domestic source of electricity. Second, it mobilizes foreign exchange and budgetary revenues to finance poverty reduction and environmental and social programs.

The domestic power system is still at an early stage of development in Lao PDR. The system consists of four networks, none of which are interconnected. Although access to the network has increased significantly in recent years, only about 61 percent of households had access to electricity by the end of 2008, and per capita electricity consumption is among the lowest in Asia. Domestic consumption currently accounts for about 85 percent of total production.

Unlocking the potential of hydropower in Lao PDR is particularly significant, given that the East Asia geographic region has the lowest percentage of exploited hydropower of any region in the world. The abundance of its hydropower resources and its central location in a rapidly growing region provide Lao PDR with a strategic advantage as power markets in the region move toward closer integration. Lao PDR is a member of the Mekong River Commission, which seeks to develop and adopt an integrated approach to river basin management in the subregion; and it has been working with other countries in the Greater Mekong subregion in developing an integrated power market.[4] Lao PDR has also been a key participant in the development of bilateral power trade, signing memoranda of understanding with Thailand (for 7,000 MW) and with Vietnam (for 5,000 MW) to export hydroelectric power. NT2 is the third dam built in Lao PDR mainly to serve the Thai market, following Nam Ngum 1 (150 MW), commissioned between 1971 and 1984, and Theun Hinboun (210 MW), commissioned in 1998. Power exports accounted for about 30 percent of total export earnings in Lao PDR in 2003. They have declined in recent years, to about 10 percent in 2007, but are expected to increase significantly after 2010, when NT2 and other large power projects come on stream, returning to about 30 percent by 2013.

Rewards and Risks for Lao PDR

The NT2 project offers a broad range of rewards, provided risks are well managed. The principal benefit of the NT2 project for Lao PDR will be the $1.95 billion (in nominal terms) of government revenues the project is expected to generate over the 25-year concession period (2009–34).[5] Mobilization of these revenues is an important part of a package of policy, administrative and developmental measures needed to increase revenue yields over the medium to long term.

The project is expected to benefit Lao PDR in many other ways as well:

- It supports the government's strategy for promoting growth and reducing poverty through private sector development, regional integration, and sound environmental and social management of the country's natural resources.
- It is helping stimulate a process of closer engagement of Lao PDR with the global community as well as an opening up of the dialogue at home.
- It is promoting familiarity with Lao PDR among a large and diverse group of investors, thereby expanding opportunities for future investments geared toward sustainable development and increasing its access to international financial markets.

- It will further integrate the country into the regional power network, as part of a broader process of regional economic integration within the framework of Lao PDR's membership in the Association of Southeast Asian Nations (ASEAN) and the ASEAN Free Trade Area (AFTA).

- It provides an opportunity to develop policies and tools that will strengthen the government's capacity to manage the country's natural resources in a sustainable manner, promote biodiversity, and protect ethnic minorities.

- With its large geographic footprint and multiple impacts, it constitutes a test case for project-specific environmental and social protection policies that have the potential to be broadly replicated throughout the country. It can also provide impetus for the development of irrigation in and around the project area.

- If successfully implemented in concert with the international community, it will demonstrate the government's commitment to sustainable development and its willingness to engage with the local population in designing and implementing a program of shared benefits at the national, regional, and local levels.

But the NT2 project also faces many development risks. Some risks arise from Lao PDR's broader development challenges. Despite the progress made in recent years, the country is still one of the poorest in East Asia, with major capacity, infrastructure, and other constraints. A big risk relates to managing project revenues. The government's share of equity in previous projects has been held by EDL, which has used part of the dividends to subsidize its operations, thereby reducing the level of government revenues.

The area of social and environmental impacts also poses severe and perhaps the most visible risks. In past projects, inadequate upfront assessment of impacts, limited resources for implementation of environmental and social mitigation activities, and insufficient monitoring and oversight have meant that the environmental and social impacts of hydropower development have often been neglected.

A further challenge is the country's limited capacity to implement sound environmental and social policies and programs beyond the hydropower sector; and in this context, whether NT2 will be seen as a project that could not be replicated due to the high standards adopted or as capable of providing approaches and solutions that contribute more broadly to the country's efforts to manage its natural resources in an environmentally and socially sustainable manner.

Engagement of the World Bank and Other Partners and Stakeholders in NT2

The long process of preparing NT2 was accompanied by a steady expansion in the range of partners and stakeholders involved. As one component of an indicative plan for developing hydropower in the Mekong basin, the project was included from its early days in discussions among neighboring countries of the Mekong River Commission and eventually in the broader discussions among the countries of the Greater Mekong subregion on the development of an integrated power market. In 1993 the partnership expanded to include the private sector and subsequently international financing entities, including export credit agencies and commercial banks, and bilateral and multilateral donors. Sometime later, international civil society and people directly affected by the project made their voices heard. The steady expansion in the range of partners and stakeholders was also accompanied by a broadening in the scope of the project, from a domestic energy project to an electricity export project and from a project severely deficient with respect to the handling of its social and environmental impacts and the management of its revenues to one with a strong emphasis on environmental and social sustainability as well as the efficient use of the revenues generated by the project.

Early Days: 1970s–1994

Although in one form or another the idea of a hydropower facility on the Nam Theun River had been raised in discussions about the development of the Mekong basin since the early 1970s, a specific project was not proposed until the 1980s. Originally, the project was conceived to provide domestic energy. In early 1988 a World Bank mission recommended that the government select NT2 for a full feasibility study. As discussions continued, the purpose of NT2 shifted from a hydropower project supplying energy to the domestic market to one that would export energy to neighboring countries.

The World Bank sent several missions to Lao PDR in the early 1990s to explore the feasibility of the project. As the potential magnitude and size of the project came to be recognized, these missions began to focus more intensively on the environmental and social aspects of NT2, including its impacts on the catchment area, the people living on the plateau, who would need to be resettled, and on downstream consequences for communities and the environment.

Second Phase: 1994–97

The developers initially sought financing from commercial banks. However, because of the risks associated with dam construction and uncertainties about the political commitment and governance capacities of the government, few were willing to consider the requests without some type of guarantee from an international financial institution. The Asian Development Bank (ADB) initially decided not to participate, because of potential overexposure in Lao PDR and in hydropower projects in general. The developers and the government were reluctant to approach the World Bank, believing that its stringent requirements and conditions would slow progress and make the project financially infeasible. Without another source of international support, however, after more than 11 months of deliberation, the developers and the government decided to approach the World Bank in 1994.

In 1995 the World Bank conducted a major technical review of NT2. This mission appreciated the technical strengths of the project but identified serious financial, environmental, and social issues that the government and the developers would have to address in order to make the project acceptable for approval. The following year, several studies were conducted to explore these issues and their implications. The firm of Lahmeyer and Worley studied alternatives to NT2 for hydropower. Louis Berger International conducted an economic impact study, and the International Union for Conservation of Nature (IUCN), together with the Wildlife Conservation Society, developed an environmental and social action plan for the watershed and corridor areas.

Because of what it thought were costly delays in obtaining needed international guarantees for the project, the original lead developer (Transfield) withdrew from the project in 1996. It sold its shares to Electricité de France (EdF), which became the new lead developer, and to the Electricity Generating Public Company of Thailand (EGCO). Two other Thai companies that had initially been members of the consortium also sold their shares to EGCO.

Setbacks: 1997–2001

An unforeseen complication in the late 1990s set back progress on NT2. The financial crisis that spread through Asia in 1997 led to declining demand for power in Thailand and liquidity problems at several Lao companies. As a result, the viability of the project once again came into question. The Asian financial crisis made it difficult to move ahead until financial uncertainties could be assessed, but the World Bank continued low-level participation through small bridging activities.

At the same time, the IUCN and the World Bank supported the formation of an independent body, the World Commission on Dams (WCD), to review the impacts, particularly on the poor, and risks associated with large infrastructure projects such as NT2. The WCD, an international, multi-stakeholder entity, reviewed the complex and often controversial issues related to, and the development impacts of, large dams and examined alternative approaches for water resources and energy development. Its report, completed in 2000, became the reference point through which external stakeholders, especially environmental nongovernmental organizations and international civil society organizations, critiqued the NT2 project and the World Bank.

By the start of the new millennium, the World Bank had undertaken a significant restructuring, putting more staff in the field and renewing its focus on poverty reduction. It had also renewed its emphasis on infrastructure for growth and poverty reduction, following almost a decade of disengagement in large-scale infrastructure projects. Under the new approach, which evolved into the new Water Resources Sector Strategy (2003), approval of large-scale infrastructure projects by the World Bank's Board of Directors depends not only on assurances that the government can manage revenue effectively but also on other criteria, including the government's capacity to reduce poverty, improve governance, and implement sound environmental and social safeguards. Preparation of NT2 and plans for its implementation, monitoring, and evaluation also had to satisfy an array of international civil society stakeholders that had become empowered by the World Bank's commitment to engage with civil society.

Reengagement: 2001–05

The World Bank actively reentered the NT2 project in 2001, after the financial situation in most Asian countries stabilized. In order to meet the broader goals outlined above, it adopted a new business approach to NT2, formally embodied in the decision framework negotiated between the World Bank and the government of Lao PDR in 2001. This framework was subsequently embraced by other multilateral donors and financiers, including the ADB (which signified its interest in supporting the project in 2003), the Agence Française du Développement (AFD), the European Investment Bank (EIB), and the Nordic Investment Bank (NIB) as well as by private financiers and most other stakeholders.

The framework consisted of three pillars. Under its terms (a) the government was to implement a development strategy and program characterized by concrete performance on poverty reduction and environmental protection; (b) the project developer and the government were to ensure that the technical, financial, and economic aspects of the project and the design and implementation of safeguard policies were of a standard acceptable to the World Bank; and (c) the government was to obtain broad support from international donors and civil society for the country's development strategy and the NT2 project itself. The framework included a sharper focus on the project's potential to help reduce poverty and improve environmental management through efficient and transparent revenue management arrangements. Given that Lao PDR is one of the poorest countries in Southeast Asia, with weak human capacity, governance, institutions and physical infrastructure, meeting these goals represented a formidable challenge.

As the new business approach was launched, the World Bank Group stepped up its capacity to deliver NT2. Measures focused on improving team organization, enhancing communications, and strengthening oversight. A strong project team was mobilized within the World Bank, and a project oversight group was established at the Bank's regional management level to guide the team. External independent expert oversight groups—including the International Advisory Group, which reported to the World Bank's president as to how the organization was performing its role relating to the project, and the Environmental and Social Panel of Experts and the Dam Safety Review Panel, both of which advised the government—played active roles. In July 2003, the project suffered a serious setback, when the lead developer, EdF, withdrew from the project, primarily for internal reasons not related to the project's viability. The governments of Lao PDR and Thailand coordinated efforts to lobby the French government to support EdF's reengagement in the project. Following several months of delicate dialogue, including correspondence between heads of state, the Nam Theun 2 Power Company (NTPC) signed a power purchase agreement with the Electricity Generating Authority of Thailand (EGAT). NTPC, the public-private partnership consortium with shareholders comprising the developers (75 percent equity) and the government of Lao PDR (25 percent equity), then began to coordinate a project financing package, which ultimately depended on World Bank Group approval of the project and a loan guarantee.

By 2004 the government had completed its Poverty Reduction Strategy Paper, with support from the World Bank, the ADB, and the International Monetary Fund, and had made progress on reforming public finance management and other aspects of the first pillar of the decision framework. On the second pillar, much progress had also been made on ensuring that project standards, including standards for the environmental and social aspects of the project, were acceptable to the financing partners, although differences remained regarding the approach to various issues, for example the treatment of downstream impacts. To address the third pillar of the decision framework— obtaining broad support from international donors and civil society for the country's development strategy and the NT2 project itself—the World Bank, other donors, the developers, and the government engaged in an intensive process of information sharing, discussion, and debate. This process culminated in a series of international workshops held in Bangkok, Paris, Tokyo, Washington, and Vientiane to provide major stakeholders with information on NT2 and to solicit the views of international civil society organizations on the project. The design and location of these workshops were driven by the dynamics of the dialogue about the project. In projects with a similar context, such workshops can be highly useful.

Project assessment was marked by debate, disagreement, and tension among the various partners and stakeholders. Some of the tension reflected substantive differences of view on the standards to be met by the project. For example, on the adequacy of local consultations in relation to the World Bank's standard of "meaningful" consultations, the developers and government were satisfied with the initial set of meetings with local communities, whereas critics argued that they offered only one-way flows of information and were often misunderstood by the communities. Another key point of contention between the developers and the World Bank was the treatment of downstream impacts and the inclusion of mitigation measures in the project's base budget. These tensions also reflected the different expectations that participants in the project had of the World Bank's role. Developers and government officials, all of whom reluctantly sought international financial guarantees, knew that the World Bank would bear a heavier burden in terms of analytical work, but they looked to the World Bank Group as a deal maker. But in endeavoring to ensure that the government and developers met international standards in the design of the project, the assessment of its risks, and the implementation of policies for applying safeguards, the World Bank was often seen to be focusing on the deal breakers that would delay or prohibit its participation in NT2.

Project Approval and Financing, March/April 2005

Despite these difficulties, in 2005 the financing partners' project appraisal for NT2 was completed, and the World Bank was satisfied that the government had met the decision framework objectives. The World Bank's Board approved the NT2 project on March 31, 2005; ADB's Board approved the project on April 4, 2005; and other partners also approved the project. Approval of NT2 confirmed the credibility of the new business approach and demonstrated the World Bank's renewed interest in investing more heavily in large-scale infrastructure, including in the hydropower sector.

At $1.45 billion (including $200 million in contingent financing), the NT2 project represented a huge financing challenge, which was met through cooperative, complementary efforts tapping public and private resources. NT2 remains the largest foreign investment in Lao PDR to date. At the time, it represented the world's largest private cross-border power financing; and it remains one of the largest internationally financed independent power projects in Asia since the financial crisis of the late 1990s. The financing process brought invaluable experience and exposure to Lao PDR, widening possibilities for more foreign direct investments.

The World Bank Group used a range of instruments to address the cross-sectoral complexities of the project and to support the new business approach. Three project instruments provided direct funding. A $20 million International Development Association (IDA) grant—the Nam Theun 2 Social and Environment Project (NTSEP)—helped fund a portion of the government's equity in the NTPC and the management of the social and environmental impacts and independent monitoring and evaluation of the NT2 project. An IDA partial risk guarantee of $42 million covered a syndicated commercial loan to NTPC. Guarantees from the Multilateral Investment Guarantee Agency (MIGA) of about $90 million for a syndicated commercial loan as well as an equity investment in NTPC covered political risks in Thailand (the external buyer of NT2 electricity) and Lao PDR. Both strategy-level and technical staff dialogue on policies and institutional reform addressed the total package of outcomes expected from this mega-project, as reflected in the project's legal framework.

In addition to the World Bank, many other institutions, including ADB and AFD, provided financial support for the project (table 1.1). ADB supported NT2 through a direct loan of $50 million, a political risk guarantee (covering $42 million of principal), and a public sector loan of $20 million to the government.

Table 1.1 NT2 Final Project Financing Plan

Source of financing	Amount of financing		
	Millions of dollars	Millions of Thai baht	Total financing (dollars at exchange rate of 40.1 baht per dollar)
Export credit agency facility	200.0		200.0
CoFACE (France)	136.0		136.0
EKN (Sweden)	29.0		29.0
GIEK (Norway)	35.0		35.0
IDA political risk guarantee facility	42.0		42.0
ADB ordinary capital resources facility	50.0		50.0
ADB political risk guarantee facility	42.0		42.0
MIGA political risk guarantee facility	42.0		42.0
AFD facility	30.0		30.0
NIB facility	34.0		34.0
Proparco facility	30.0		30.0
Thai Exim facility	30.0		30.0
Commercial bank facility		20,000.0	500.0
Total long-term debt	500.0	20,000.0	1,000.0
Tranche A	450.0	18,000.0	900.0
Tranche B	50.0	2,000.0	100.0
Total equity	445.2	190.5	450.0
Tranche A	345.2	190.5	350.0
Tranche B	100.0		100.0
Private equity	332.7	190.5	337.5
Government equity[a]	112.5		112.5
ADB loan	16.1		
AFD grant	6.2		
EIB loan	41.0		
IDA grant	20.0		
Government contribution	29.2		
Total base and contingent financing	945.2	20,190.5	1,450.0

Source: Joint World Bank–Asian Development Bank Update report, June 22, 2005.
a. Full loan amounts are slightly higher to cover interest during construction.

Five Years On, November 2010

Following approval, the project quickly broke ground in November 2005. The construction and electromechanical works are now complete, and generation of electricity has commenced. It is remarkable that the 54-month construction period faced only a small delay of four months. The environmental and social programs operate on a longer timeframe, and their implementation is ongoing. The two programs faced some start-up delays and implementation snags in the early days, but they are now on track. Both programs will continue to face many risks and challenges, which are inherent in these types of interventions. The important thing is that the government of Lao PDR, NTPC, and the World Bank and other international financing institutions are all committed to ensuring that the promised outcomes are realized over the concession period.

Introduction to the Chapters

The chapters that follow describe the process of project preparation and identify lessons learned from the project. They provide readers with perspective on the country development context, the scope and depth of project preparation activities, stakeholder objectives, the importance of partnerships and common goals, and progress on implementation.

Chapters 2–4 are structured around the three pillars of the decision framework underpinning the World Bank's new business approach to NT2 project preparation. They describe how Lao PDR got ready for the project; how the project was prepared, taking the country context into account; and how stakeholders worked together during the preparation process. Chapter 5 provides some additional perspectives on the communications aspects of project preparation. Chapter 6 presents broader lessons from cross-cutting challenges encountered during project preparation that straddle more than one pillar of the decision framework. Chapter 7 provides a snapshot of project implementation. Chapter 8 provides an assessment from the field of NT2's role in strengthening Lao PDR's development prospects by acting as a driver of change.

Chapter 2: Lao PDR Gets Ready for NT2

Chapter 2 describes how the first pillar of the decision framework—getting Lao PDR ready for NT2—was implemented. Uncertainty surrounding the untested country environment meant that foreign investors needed not only the comfort of a World Bank guarantee but also an acceptable country framework that signaled that the country was ready for broader reform to achieve its growth and poverty reduction goals. Such a framework required that NT2 be embedded in a national poverty reduction strategy and used as a catalyst for sustainable economic reform and strengthened institutions. It was also essential that a program of time-bound economic reforms be developed and implemented to build credibility in the capacity of the government to implement structural change. The framework included a major focus on strengthening public institutions, especially those responsible for revenue management, in order to ensure that resources were allocated in line with poverty reduction priorities and to diminish the risk of corruption. In the case of NT2 revenues, the framework also included an innovative program for linking project revenues tightly to specific poverty reduction and environmental conservation programs.

Homi Kharas and Rosa Alonso i Terme, the chapter's authors, argue that the World Bank's development policy lending instrument served well as both an implementation and a monitoring tool for supporting the development of such a framework and measuring progress. This instrument was supported by high-quality analytical work that was owned by the government and most other stakeholders and strengthened by effective communications and consultations. The instrument helped ensure that the World Bank and other financiers judged the government's commitment and capacity to deliver on policy reform and poverty reduction on the basis of its track record, with financiers prepared to walk away from support to the project if critical conditions were not fulfilled.

According to the authors, the World Bank rightly focused on principles of engagement, not specific policies, and provided enough space for flexibility and government ownership. Rather than trying to bypass local institutions and systems, the World Bank used the process of engagement for constructive support of strengthened country systems and processes, even when implementation was difficult because of limited domestic capacity. Performance fell short in identifying areas of weak capacity early on and designing a capacity-building strategy to address them. Neither financial nor technical support for capacity building was adequate for the challenge. The World Bank's toolkit and professional resources for effectively supporting capacity building lacked depth, and it was difficult to persuade the government to seriously engage in capacity building until the Bank committed to supporting NT2, a commitment that took time to materialize.

Given the high visibility of the NT2 project, developing a certain level of trust and fostering stakeholder partnerships was essential to moving forward on strengthening the development framework. The World Bank team's understanding of and sensitivity to the political and cultural context in Lao PDR helped it devise the right engagement strategy and behave in an appropriate manner. Sensitivity to the government decision-making process was a critical ingredient in the eventual development of a relationship of mutual trust between the World Bank and the government.

The authors note the importance of bringing on board a broad-based management team early on, engaging management at the highest level of the World Bank by employing the decision framework approach to report progress, and encouraging staff to show flexibility and willingness to take risks. They also note that the speed of project processing reflected the time needed for the World Bank to carry out due diligence, the government to deliver on its reform agenda, and stakeholders to establish trust.

Chapter 3: The Project Is Prepared

Chapter 3 examines the second pillar of the decision framework: getting the project ready for Lao PDR. As formidable as they were, the technical and engineering challenges of the project had more readily available and less controversial solutions than other aspects of preparation. The authors of chapter 3—Teresa Serra, Mark Segal, and Ram Chopra—therefore examine the challenges involved in handling the more difficult aspects of the project, including social and environmental, economic, and financial issues.

Working closely with ADB and AFD and heeding the lessons of past dam projects, the World Bank conducted a thorough upfront assessment of environmental and social issues and drafted a robust implementation plan detailing the necessary institutional arrangements, budget oversight, and contingency measures for effective implementation of the environmental and social management plan. NT2 presented a unique opportunity for learning about and refining the World Bank's and other partners' approach to environmental and social safeguards in large infrastructure operations.

The large scale of the civil works meant that NT2 had widespread regional and cumulative environmental and social impacts. It triggered all 10 of the World Bank's safeguard policies. Impact analysis and mitigation planning had to be comprehensive, including planning for the resettlement of about 6,200 people living on the plateau. High-quality information gathering and analysis followed by comprehensive and detailed plan formulation in consultation with all the stakeholders involved was critical. The government, NTPC, and other stakeholders initially balked at the demands placed on them, claiming that the World Bank and its partners were continuously expanding both the geographical scope and the thematic coverage of the analysis, "shifting the goalposts" without clearly defining an acceptable set of requirements. For their part, civil society organizations believed that the environmental and social analyses were insufficiently comprehensive and that some essential potential problems or groups of people who would be affected by the project were ignored.

Teresa Serra identifies several lessons on a number of substantive environmental and social issues: defining project boundaries and area of influence; ensuring income restoration and livelihood enhancement, with special attention to vulnerable groups; balancing biodiversity conservation, protection of wildlife habitats, and local development objectives; and addressing downstream risks. She then discusses lessons pertaining to cross-cutting and process issues: addressing uncertainty through budgets and legal instruments; establishing realistic and responsive institutional arrangements; engaging in participatory consultation and transparent communication throughout the project cycle; and engaging in internal and external project monitoring.

To be more effective, the author stresses that the World Bank needs to agree with the developer and the government early regarding the key elements of the approach to addressing the project's environmental and social issues. It is also important to recognize that it is not possible to identify all requirements upfront and that flexibility to adapt to new information is essential. In this regard, the advice of respected independent outside experts, including the International Advisory Group, the Environmental and Social Panel of Experts, and the Dam Safety Review Panel, can be invaluable. The author also notes that, especially in the case of public-private partnerships, it is critical that the World Bank understand the extent to which the project can be called upon to address broader developmental issues that are associated with, but not directly linked to, the project. In this regard the use of parallel complementary operations (such as the Lao Environment and Social Project) is an approach that should be replicated in similar cases.

Four broad questions about project economics were raised during NT2 project preparation:

- Was the project needed by the proposed commissioning date (if at all)?
- Was the project consistent with the least-cost strategy for expanding Thailand's power supply?

- Would there be enough value added from NT2's power production to, at a minimum, compensate the project's environmental and social impacts in Lao PDR?
- How likely was the project to remain economically viable over time?

In chapter 3, Mark Segal explores those questions in some depth, reaching positive conclusions about all of them.

The chapter also discusses risk analysis. Even robust analytics may not fully incorporate the possible extent of some uncertainties: four years after the development of the major assumptions underlying this work, the world evolved in ways that no one dreamed of, let alone considered and dismissed as too improbable to analyze. Given this experience, the author asks: Are conventional views about reasonable boundaries of risk analysis adequate for analyzing a range of future outcomes? How useful is it to depend on forecasts, however elaborate and whatever the assumption ranges, for project evaluation?

With respect to the project's financial package, Ram Chopra applauds the quality and sophistication of its design. He notes that the World Bank's financial partners appreciated the professionalism and expertise of World Bank staff and the value of its environmental and social standards. In fact, with minor variations, they would like to see World Bank standards applied in future projects, even when the World Bank is not directly involved. They also appreciated that through the successful financial closure of NT2, the World Bank raised the creditworthiness of Lao PDR, making it possible for international lenders and private developers to seriously consider taking Lao risk for future private sector projects without guarantees from the World Bank (and in some cases without risk mitigation by other institutions).

On the negative side, partners criticized the World Bank for failing to understand the constraints under which the private sector operates. To address this concern, the World Bank needs to ensure that staff members are sensitive to the context within which the private sector operates.

Improving process efficiency is also critical. Early in the preparation process, the financial and other costs that have to be borne by the developers must be clearly spelled out and agreed to. The private sector needs more predictable budget and cost estimates up front; it has serious problems with open-ended commitments.

Coordination between multiple experts and missions needs improvement, so that different messages are not conveyed to partners. Ensuring the predictability of expectations and avoiding the perception of "shifting goalposts" is critical. The information flow, particularly among partners, must be well managed to provide timely information in a manner stakeholders can understand.

The World Bank needs to consider more carefully the balance between its financing role and the policy leverage it exercises, in recognition of the fact that its use of policy leverage imposes costs as well as benefits for borrower and developers. In all large, high-visibility, and contentious projects, the World Bank needs to strike a better balance between the need for continuous senior management oversight and the need to maintain the authority of the team manager with respect to both internal and external players.

Chapter 3 provides some useful suggestions on how to improve the World Bank's business model. Detailed risk identification early in the project preparation cycle and development of risk-mitigation measures to cover all risks lead to a risk-avoidance strategy rather than an appropriate risk-management strategy. With that in mind, for all large infrastructure projects, the World Bank may wish to address risk management in a two-stage decision process. In the first stage, early in the project cycle, the World Bank would decide in principle whether or not to fund a project. This decision could be based on an up-front assessment of risks and rewards and the practicality of mitigating risks to an acceptable level. If positive, such a decision should be followed by a decision framework that includes a set of detailed (yet flexible) monitorable achievement targets, anchored in a two- to three-year work program, supported by donor and government budgets, with work-sharing arrangements with financiers and partners. Such a framework, if implemented to the satisfaction of the World Bank, would lead to the Bank's ultimate decision on involvement in the project. This approach would signal interest by the World Bank earlier; establish transparent, measurable, and monitorable goalposts; and prompt the developer to commit resources to design safeguards sooner than was the case in NT2. It would also help create an environment in which the government would be more likely to agree to jump-start capacity building earlier, at both the national and the project levels. For the World Bank, such an approach would reduce the risks of providing signals on its ultimate involvement too early, without having completed its due diligence

From the World Bank's point of view, NT2 is a good news/bad news story. The good news is that its hard work and high standards led to the successful introduction of Lao PDR to the private international markets and opened up possibilities for private developers to seriously consider large infrastructure projects in other low-income East Asian countries with weak creditworthiness.

The bad news is that the World Bank is seen as a high-cost/high-hassle partner of last resort. There is therefore a critical need to reduce the costs the private sector incurs for doing business with the World Bank. Doing so will require the World Bank to better understand the constraints under which the private sector works.

Chapter 4: Working with Stakeholders

Chapter 4, by Nazir Ahmad, examines the challenges of engaging a varied and changing roster of stakeholders—including people affected by the project, the government, developers, and critics of the project—and draws lessons about stakeholder relations from the experiences of NT2 preparation. It first looks at the process of soliciting the views of people affected by the project through local consultations. Early efforts were one-way monologues that transmitted technical information but did little to elicit surfacing of uncomfortable questions or opinions. These shortcomings were addressed after 2003, when a new methodology elicited fuller and more unscripted feedback. To ensure that the consultation process was robust and meaningful, the international financial institutions engaged a well-respected international social anthropologist, with expertise on Lao PDR, to monitor the efforts. The consultation efforts successfully brought forward a broad array of opinions, which were incorporated into the project design and approach; however, the array of livelihood options (which were overwhelming to some resettlers) could have been simplified, and the findings of the consultations could have been more fully harvested by better cataloguing, using, and archiving the information collected.

The author stresses the importance of local consultations beginning early in the project development cycle, so that adequate baseline information can be collected. Consultation efforts should be tailored to the affected population to improve understanding and remove barriers to expression of opinions, with an independent monitor engaged to verify the robustness of the efforts. People affected by the project should be segmented (based on issues, characteristics, and concerns, for example), with clear ground rules put in place to prevent authority figures from dominating discussions or compromising candor.

Chapter 4 also examines the cultivation of meaningful engagement with the government. In the early years of project development, before 1999, the government's role in NT2 was limited, with the developer leading the efforts and government relying heavily on external advisers. The government enjoyed a cordial relationship with the developer but was relatively unfamiliar with the World Bank. There was a lack of clear understanding of each party's objectives, constraints, requirements, and expectations. As NT2 was recast as more of a development (rather than simply a stand-alone hydropower) project, the government took on a more active leadership role. Through preparation of the country's poverty reduction strategy, appraisal of several related projects, and various other interactions, the World Bank and the government cultivated greater mutual trust and confidence over time.

Several strategic lessons emerge from this experience. To avoid tensions down the road, early assessment should be made to determine the fundamental objectives of all key stakeholders, as well as their organizational arrangements and capacity constraints. The government, the World Bank, and counterparts should seek common understanding about risks and rewards. To clarify expectations, they should discuss what requirements, provisions, and standards are nonnegotiable, and why, and develop a common, agreed-upon understanding of risks and rewards.

The relationship between the World Bank and the developer was strained at times, because of differing and sometimes conflicting interests. This was compounded by multiple points of contact with the World Bank that did not always present consistent messages and by exchanges of information that were not always as timely as desired. Closure was eventually reached, by diligently working through differences, but the process was at times contentious and some opportunities for capacity building may have been lost in the interest of staying on schedule.

From the beginning, NT2 was a lightning rod for criticism; the debate on dams and NT2 had a long and contentious history. The World Bank had to be on guard against reputational risk from misinformation. Over time, it came to use communications as a strategic lever to influence the debate on NT2. The author lauds as innovative and valuable the use of proactive and constructive communications to ensure that balanced and factual information was made available to all stakeholders, including critics of NT2. While acknowledging that many critics have deep-rooted views that were unlikely to be changed, he notes that some opportunities for constructive engagement with critics may have been missed because of misperceptions (for example, the belief that each party's view was firm and unified internally, leaving no room for alternative views). He gives critics credit for offering a number of helpful insights, posing critical questions that helped identify issues that had not received adequate attention, and prompting deeper examination of the World Bank's and the developer's assumptions and predispositions, but he notes that maintaining constructive dialogue was difficult. In the future, the World Bank should place even greater emphasis on understanding the underlying concerns of its critics, even if the criticisms are based on ideological grounds.

On controversial projects, a proactive and two-way communications strategy should be in place from the start. That strategy should demonstrate transparency and offer meaningful, accurate, timely, and accessible information to all stakeholders. Views should be elicited from the full range of interested parties, striking a healthy balance between listening to issues and defending against incorrect information. Specific but flexible guidelines should be established for distinguishing legitimate concerns from efforts to stall or halt a project. A system should be in place to catalogue and evaluate criticisms and track responses. Negative press should be anticipated, internal efforts should manage expectations and reactions, and spokespeople should be trained to handle the range of issues. International workshops should be designed, on a case-by-case basis, so that views across a broad range of participants are elicited; information should be provided well ahead of the discussion, and independent moderators and facilitation techniques should be used to stimulate constructive dialogue. Following the workshops, evaluations should be undertaken to determine if the design was effective.

The government and developers found the World Bank's decision-making mechanisms to be diffuse and unpredictable and its focus on risks excessive. They were frustrated, particularly over the perceived shifting of goalposts (for example, the number and scope of mandated analytical studies) as project preparation ensued. The author suggests that the World Bank clearly communicate its decision basis to all stakeholders and clarify priorities and requirements up front, based on transparent rationale. Having a small team on the developer side coordinate multiple studies based on an agreed and prioritized master list would help to better allocate resources; and more centralized project management on the World Bank side could have better facilitated and coordinated information requests across the various sectors.

Chapter 5: The Communications Challenge

Chapter 5 provides some further reflections on the communications challenge for NT2, with a particular focus on the role played by the World Bank. It describes the unusual role that communications played throughout the assessment, planning, and implementation of NT2. Coming after a spate of controversial—and sometimes failed or withdrawn—projects, NT2 was seen by many supporters and critics as a test case. It inherited legacy issues, including concerns that any major infrastructure project would be beset by external challenges to the point that the project team would be unable to perform its proper role.

According to Peter Stephens, the chapter's author, several critical factors contributed to the success of the communications operation. Among them were the establishment of the communications function as a central component of the core project team, the inclusion of communications specialists in the core project team, agreement on messages and the need for the World Bank to be clear on its position at all times, a commitment to transparency from the earliest stages of project consideration, and the government's embrace of quick and open communications from its own offices.

A particularly interesting aspect of the NT2 communications effort was the extent to which it differed from earlier projects in dealing with NGOs that were entrenched in their opposition to the project. Peter Stephens argues that the positions of such critics were well known and immovable. The World Bank scrutinized and responded to their questions—but it made sure it did not become sidetracked or allow itself to be defined by avowed opponents of the project.

The author concludes that the communications component of NT2 can and should be adapted to other complex infrastructure projects. Projects that undervalue the role of communications expose themselves to needless and expensive risks.

Chapter 6: Some Cross-Cutting Lessons

In chapter 6, experts from the Duke Center for International Development (DCID) draw cross-cutting lessons for the World Bank—based largely on the findings of chapters 2–4—in six areas:

- Transforming NT2 into a social development and poverty reduction project
- Building government capacity and trust between the World Bank and the government
- Applying the World Bank's environmental and social safeguard policies to the project

- Managing project financial risks
- Constructively engaging stakeholders
- Overseeing and managing NT2.

To help the country ready itself for NT2, the project had to be complemented by a program of broader development interventions—going well beyond a typical project. The World Bank helped the government improve transparency and accountability, thereby strengthening its institutions and processes. The authors endorse the adoption of the new business process under which NT2 project preparation was linked to the government's progress on implementing plans and policies for reducing poverty and improving environmental management, concluding that this linkage was key to nurturing the growth of mutual trust and accountability that facilitated progress in all areas. The authors note that sensitivities to the cultural and political context of Lao PDR; an enhanced field presence by World Bank staff; and emphasis on openness, respect, and consistency of messages helped deepen trust over the years, as did symbolic and substantive signs of commitment by high levels in the government and the World Bank. Nevertheless, a fuller and earlier understanding of the constraints of all key stakeholders, with clear delineation of nonnegotiable requirements and standards, would have been beneficial, and capacity building could have been more comprehensive with earlier and better alignment of objectives, measurement of specifics skills required, and more customized training.

Application of the World Bank's safeguard policies helped reduce the overall risk of the project while increasing the project's credibility with stakeholders. The creative application of environmental set-asides to "offset" inundated areas is helping ensure long-term net benefits through protection of adjacent areas. The creation of a panel of experts has been instrumental in providing guidance on environmental and social aspects, including the impetus for developing comprehensive social and environmental management plans and undertaking extensive studies in support of impact identification. Meaningful and transparent consultations, which started at the early stage of resettlement planning and continued into implementation, have been critical for identifying solutions preferred by villagers. An innovative approach adopted for needs assessment, focusing on livelihoods and vulnerabilities, is helping to ensure that Indigenous Peoples affected by the project are provided with appropriate development options.

More could have been done, however, to avoid perceptions that the World Bank was moving goalposts when analysis demonstrated a legitimate need for additional safeguard studies. Further development of a preparation framework could have helped streamline application of the safeguards by clearly delineating roles and responsibilities for all parties. Such a framework could have served as the basis for developing an explicit and integrated decision process for determining requirements for analytical studies. Early screening and scoping of environmental and social issues, carried out with stakeholder consultation, would have helped identify key issues. Having a clear single point of contact for coordination of safeguards issues would have facilitated interactions with counterparts.

The authors give high marks to the treatment of the financial risk of NT2. Comprehensive and integrated risk assessment was conducted at the outset to identify key risks and devise appropriate mitigation strategies. Creativity and innovation were critical in designing the guarantee structure, funding the government's equity in the project, and tailoring the financial package to fit the reward/risk profile of the diverse set of investors. To help mitigate criticisms and concerns, progress on governance matters needs to keep pace with project financing efforts. Sensitivity to cost considerations and burden sharing is also needed, with clear identification and agreement by all parties early in the process. The efficiency of the financing process could be improved by working with a smaller number of institutions, each carrying a larger share and being involved in the process and key decisions from early on.

Especially in the case of internationally sensitive projects, a clear strategy for effective engagement and communication (including consultations and disclosure) helps broaden understanding, enhance transparency and accountability, improve project design and implementation, and pave the way for more constructive criticism. It is also important to ensure the availability of easily accessible information that is accurate, balanced, timely, and comprehensible as a foundation for informed dialogue.

Having two separate but related projects (NT2 and the Nam Theun 2 Social and Environment Project [NTSEP]) enabled objectives to be tailored and operational flexibility to be maintained. Having a dedicated project team that included strong technical skills, keen awareness of the local political and cultural context, strong commitment to helping the country achieve its development objectives, and a good understanding of the World Bank bureaucracy was instrumental to carrying out the project preparation tasks successfully. An internal project oversight group helped the World Bank maintain an integrated and coordinated internal approach and demonstrate an institutional commitment. Nevertheless, NT2 was difficult and costly to prepare, given its various complexities and the level of due diligence undertaken. Intense involvement of senior management helped solidify internal consensus and mitigate institutional risk. But it also lengthened processing times, added to costs, and negatively affected the team's sense of independence and authority (internal and external). There is scope for attaining a better balance internally while granting the team ample latitude and retaining sufficient oversight. Externally, it is important to ensure an appropriate division of labor among project partners, tapping relative strengths, to enhance effectiveness, reduce duplication, and share workloads fairly. Agreements should be sought early on regarding the reporting requirements of the developer and government, ensuring accountability without unnecessary burden. Missions by international financial institutions should be conducted jointly to reduce disruption.

Chapter 7: Reflections on Implementation

Chapter 7, by Mara Baranson, provides a brief overview of the progress on project implementation, including some preliminary reflections on what has been learned thus far. Although NT2 was unique in many ways, many of its lessons can be tailored and adapted to other applications.

Most of the risks that materialized during implementation were foreseen and have been satisfactorily addressed; the many challenges encountered, inevitable for a project of this size and complexity, have been met with varying degrees of success. The legal framework for the project has served well in documenting obligations, commitments, and means of recourse while clarifying roles and responsibilities. More systematic capacity building could have been accomplished, but progress has been made in many areas, albeit on a learning-by-doing basis. Aid effectiveness has been enhanced through development of strong partnerships between the international financial institutions and donors, which tap synergies through complementary support. Those relationships have also had positive implications for NT2 implementation, facilitating resolution of sticky issues and coordination among the large number of parties participating in efforts such as supervision activities. The multilayered monitoring arrangements have added value in supporting risk identification and providing guidance on finding and implementing solutions to complex issues and problems. There is, nevertheless, room for streamlining to reduce the burden of multiple visits on the implementing agencies.

Chapter 8: NT2: A Transformative Endeavor

Complementing the observations in chapter 7, Patchamuthu Illangovan provides additional thoughts on the broader impact of NT2 in chapter 8. He reveals how NT2 project goals are being realized on the ground and addresses some of the challenges ahead in four areas: the development context, the hydropower facility and related infrastructure, environmental and social programs, and international support.

Achieving financial closure on NT2 in 2005 buoyed the hydropower industry worldwide. It also gave credence to the notion that Lao PDR could tap its rich water resources to address the power needs of its neighbors and eventually become the "battery of South East Asia." The project helped institutionalize public-private partnership as a business model in the country. Since the deal's closure, interest in investing in Lao hydropower has swelled, with a "hydro rush" ensuing as dam builders and contractors, power utilities, and consultants descend on the country. Moving forward must be done in a methodical and careful way, based on a sector strategy and plans, so that opportunities are pursued on the basis of sustainability, affordability, and benefit sharing.

Path-breaking and wide-reaching reforms have been achieved in public financial management in Lao PDR; reform momentum has been sustained, supported by an authorizing political environment and significant strides in implementation capacity. The government's commitment to reforms has been matched by development partners' willingness to provide technical and financial support for reform implementation. Embedding the NT2 revenue-management arrangement in the broader Public Financial Management Strengthening Program has helped keep work largely on track. The priority programs eligible to receive NT2 revenues have been identified. The challenges going forward will be to track expenditures, monitor performance, audit expenses, and continue the impressive progress toward creation of a well-developed public financial management system, so that Lao PDR can transparently and productively use the revenues from NT2 to benefit its people.

Implementing the programs that address social and environmental impacts, which involves introducing behavioral and mindset changes, has taken longer than building the dam itself. After some bumpy starts and myriad changes and adjustments, the implementers now appear fully geared up to deliver longer-term results.

The use of local consultations in building empowerment among villagers is a noteworthy achievement of the project. The NT2 resettlement process serves as a model for other hydropower projects under consideration or construction; villagers from many affected communities of other projects have asked to see and learn from the NT2 experience, a request that has been accommodated through site visits. At the same time, the development of livelihoods for the resettlers remains a difficult challenge, which is being addressed through a multipronged approach that has evolved over time as "teething" issues are addressed through adaptive management with inputs from local consultations and technical experts.

Protection of the NT2 watershed is a work in progress. The establishment and staffing of the Watershed Management and Protection Authority provides a sound foundation, but enormous challenges remain in protecting such a vast area from those who want to pilfer its riches. The author cautions that the long-term protection of the NT2 watershed will require high-level political support from the government on a continuing basis.

The work undertaken as part of the NT2 project's wildlife program—which tapped the expertise of various conservation groups and technical specialists to make important achievements in the areas of elephant management and wildlife rescue—serves as a benchmark for other hydropower projects to replicate. The activities undertaken by the developers with respect to salvage logging and biomass clearance went beyond what was originally agreed on during project design; those activities serve as a model for similar operations in other hydropower areas.

The first five years of implementation have provided a strong foundation for future efforts. Implementing the project's social and environmental programs has proved as challenging as anticipated at the time of design, and many questions remain as implementation progresses. Some positive outcomes are already evident: the government has acquired significant capacity to implement social and environmental mitigation programs, and it has demonstrated its commitment and intervened at all levels to resolve problems as they have arisen. Tapping lessons from NT2, the government is recasting its overall approach to social and environmental impact assessment and monitoring (with a new agency and a decree). At the same time, the developer is credited for its steadfast commitment to ensuring that environmental and social obligations are fully met. The author stresses the importance of the developer continuing this commitment throughout the commercial operations period, resisting the temptation to declare victory too early.

International support for NT2 has been catalyzed through meaningful sharing of information. NT2 continues to garner international attention. The government and the developers remain committed to independent monitoring of the project as well as the maintenance of an open and transparent process of sharing information with stakeholders. A very complex and layered project monitoring structure evolved as preparation progressed and implementation ensued. Each entity provides valuable inputs and responds to its mandate, outlined in various legal agreements. There is, nevertheless, considerable scope to simplify the monitoring arrangements as the operating context has changed with the start of commercial operations. In an effort to keep stakeholders informed, the developer has supported knowledge exchange, transparency, and disclosure—through various modalities, including Web sites, workshops/forums, and peer-to-peer learning activities—that go well beyond requirements. Coordination across the large number of institutions working on NT2 has been facilitated by remarkably good and constructive collaboration and cooperation by the international financial institutions. Enhanced donor funding to implement the Lao socioeconomic development plans and multidonor efforts to support implementation of government reforms have also boosted international support. The government is reaping dividends—in the form of investment, trade, aid, and knowledge—from its engagement with the international community through NT2, as trust increases while the government demonstrates that it stands behind its commitments.

NT2 has helped transform Lao PDR through new institutions and policies. The country appears to be pointed in the right direction to achieve sustainable outcomes over the longer term. It is too soon to draw final conclusions on NT2, however, because the implementation process is still unfolding.

Notes

1. Project costs include the $1.25 billion base cost plus $200 million in contingency funding.
2. The Mekong River Commission Secretariat is the operational arm of the Mekong River Commission, established by an agreement signed by the governments of Cambodia, Lao PDR, Thailand, and Vietnam on April 5, 1995. The agreement set a new mandate for the organization to cooperate in the sustainable development, use, management, and conservation of the water and related resources of the Mekong River Basin. The Mekong River Commission evolved from the Mekong Committee, formed in the 1950s to conduct long-range planning for river basin development.

3. Key elements of the NGPES were later incorporated into the National Socio-Economic Development Plan (NSEDP, 2006-10), which presents a range of priorities and programs to guide progress towards the country's development goals.

4. The Greater Mekong subregion includes Cambodia, Lao PDR, Myanmar, Thailand, Vietnam, and Yunnan and Guangxi provinces of China.

5. The first test energy generation took place in June 2009. NT2 started commercial operations in April 2010.

CHAPTER 2

Lao PDR Gets Ready for NT2

Rosa Alonso i Terme and Homi Kharas

The economic landscape within which Nam Theun 2 (NT2) was prepared was not a promising one. Lao PDR is a small, isolated, low-income country with much room for improvement in its policy and institutional environment, as evidenced by its Country Policy and Institutional Assessment (CPIA) score and governance ratings (Governance Matters IV).[1] Its track record of implementing economic reforms since they were first launched in the 1980s has been uneven. Although the reforms, which started moving the economy from central planning toward a market-based system, yielded impressive growth rates, Lao PDR still faced significant structural risks when NT2 was being prepared. The pace of reform stalled after the East Asian crisis of 1997/98. Timber exports, which had been based on unsustainable logging, started to fall in 2004, and it was not clear whether the country's garment exports could thrive once the international quota system was removed in 2005.

High uncertainty over the untested country environment meant that in order to move forward with a major investment like NT2, foreign investors needed not only the comfort of a World Bank guarantee but also an acceptable country framework that signaled that the country was ready for broader change in order to achieve its growth and poverty reduction goals. This was the context within which the decision was made to move forward with NT2 only once a development framework was in place that would produce concrete results in poverty reduction and environmental protection.

Given the country's weak institutions, many questioned whether the development of natural resources was the best path toward poverty reduction.

The contributions of Adrian Fozzard and Jennifer Thomson are gratefully acknowledged.

The World Bank had experience with many low-income countries that had lost the opportunity to productively use the wealth generated by resource exploitation—through corruption, poor governance, and limited economic diversification. There was much fear that a similar fate would befall Lao PDR unless progress with economic and institutional reform continued and, in particular, unless the country was able to develop and implement a sound development strategy with a focus on poverty reduction.

The risk of slippage on reforms during implementation was of special concern to the World Bank. In most development projects it supports, the World Bank retains significant leverage over project implementation by controlling the amount of aid it provides. In contrast, under NT2 the Bank's leverage would be much diminished once the financial guarantee had been issued. Would the Bank's traditional instrument—conditionality of aid—be effective in this case?

The World Bank's strategy was to try to turn the natural resource curse on its head. Because it was a priority project for the government and there was a sufficient amount of political will, the process of engagement around NT2 could be used as a catalyst for sustainable economic reform and strengthened institutions. Natural resource wealth would then be used to promote better governance rather than, potentially, exacerbating poor governance and corruption.

Achievement of this goal required a very different project design and strategy from those adopted in similar projects in the past. Unlike in other mega hydro projects, the World Bank's engagement with the government would go beyond narrow project technical issues and focus on policies and processes to deliver greater transparency and accountability, growth, and poverty reduction. Strategy and project design, however, would have to be underpinned by a strong government commitment to implementation.

The World Bank strategy for helping the country ready itself for NT2 had three components:

- Linkage of the project firmly to a comprehensive government-led poverty reduction strategy
- A program of time-bound economic reforms, monitored by the Bank, to build credibility in the capacity of the government to implement structural change and to make any reversal of strategy unlikely
- Efforts to strengthen public institutions, especially on revenue management, in order to ensure that resources would be allocated in line with

poverty reduction priorities and to diminish the risk of corruption and other symptoms of the natural resource curse.

Judgments on each of these three components were made to ensure that the country was ready for NT2. They were the result of a step-by-step process of confidence- and credibility-building spanning 2002–05.

Poverty Reduction and Reform Progress

Rapid growth in the 1990s had already delivered some poverty reduction in Lao PDR. Between 1997 and 2002, the percentage of the population living below the national poverty line fell from 39 percent to 33 percent. Lao PDR was also making quick progress in some key areas that improve the well-being of the poor and lay the groundwork for long-term income poverty reduction, such as education and health. It had one of the most egalitarian distributions of income in the world (with a Gini coefficient of 0.35) and a high degree of political stability.

As in all low-income countries, however, there were significant problems in both the education and the health sectors. In 2001 only 1.9 percent of GDP was allocated from the budget to education. After the 1997 crisis, public spending on health collapsed to just 1 percent of GDP, with recurrent spending taking the brunt of the cuts. This low level of expenditure had severe impacts on both the coverage and the quality of education and health programs.

The serious problem of poverty in Lao PDR had to be tackled through a number of strategies that supported the progress already underway and, in particular, improved access to good-quality public services. Growth itself would not be enough; attacking poverty would require greater and more-efficient public expenditure focused on poverty reduction as well as improved governance. The source of growth could be as important as the level of aggregate growth, with growth in agriculture possibly generating far more poverty reduction than growth in industry. Overall, an educated and healthier population would be the critical underpinning for pro-poor growth. Such a strategy required more resources for social services.

The government had slowly been moving down the path of economic reform and greater openness since 1986. Once the new policy direction started to take shape, the World Bank began to engage with the government on economic reform, providing a Structural Adjustment Credit in 1992. The pace of reform slowed in the aftermath of the East Asian crisis, causing the cancellation of this loan. The structural reform process was restarted in 1999, after macroeconomic stabilization was achieved; the World Bank supported economic reform through new structural adjustment loans, which have been in place since 2002.

Since 2002 a structural adjustment program—supported by a Financial Management and Adjustment Credit (FMAC) and subsequent Poverty Reduction Support Operations (PRSOs)—has been used to support the government in continuing down the path of reform and, hence, to prepare the ground for NT2. The importance of implementing the reforms agreed to under the FMAC was clear to the government, which greatly enhanced the World Bank's leverage in supporting reformers within the government and the reform agenda as a whole. The government implemented all of the reforms promised in the FMAC—albeit with a one-year delay—creating a track record of delivering on economic reform. This record critically influenced the World Bank's assessment of whether the government could deliver on economic reform and hence of the desirability of NT2.

Other important signs also suggested that Lao PDR was slowly emerging from its historical isolation and moving down the road of regional integration and increasing openness. In 1997 it joined the Association of Southeast Asian Nations (ASEAN) and the ASEAN Free Trade Area (AFTA). In 2003 it signed a preferential trading agreement with the United States, which granted it normal trade relations status in 2005. There was thus enough fertile ground in both poverty reduction and economic reform for the World Bank to build on, in the hope that supporting the government's ongoing reform efforts would yield a "good enough" policy and institutional environment to allow it to approve NT2.

A Holistic Approach Grounded on Poverty Reduction Strategies

The World Bank decided that the best approach to maximizing the impact of NT2 on poverty reduction would be to nest it in a holistic approach to the country's poverty reduction strategy. Under the aegis of the Poverty Reduction Strategy Paper (PRSP) process, in 2003/04 the government developed a National Growth and Poverty Eradication Strategy (NGPES). This framework paper spelled out a long-term vision for development, based on the goal of exiting least developed country status by 2020. The NGPES defined various targets with 44 related indicators to be monitored over time, including on poverty reduction, agricultural growth, health, education, and governance. It set a target of 7 percent annual economic growth as the basis for achieving these targets. Because of its projected contribution to both growth and government revenues, NT2 was an integral component of the NGPES.

In content and process, the NGPES represented a major step forward. Its successful articulation was among the first indications that the government was able to manage the broader reform effort necessary for NT2 to succeed. The government owned the NGPES; World Bank, Asian Development Bank (ADB), and International Monetary Fund (IMF) staff played supporting, not central, roles.

The World Bank decided to support the NGPES through a holistic approach to the country's development strategy. The 2005 country assistance strategy for Lao PDR, developed by the Bank and endorsed by the Government, showed how the whole Bank program, including support for NT2, would be integrated with the NGPES. This approach was reflected in four main ways:

- A series of PRSOs or budget support operations
- A systemic approach to public finance management reform
- A supporting Financial Management Capacity-Building Credit (FMCBC) and, later, a Public Expenditure Management Strengthening Program (PEMSP)
- Analytical work to monitor the impact of public spending on poverty reduction

The strategy focused on three areas:

- Enhancing the transparency, participation, poverty focus, and results orientation of government processes and policies through the NGPES and successor plans
- Supporting economic reform through the FMAC and the PRSOs
- Strengthening public finance management through the FMCBC and the PEMSP.

What the strategy did not include is as significant as what it did include. In particular, the World Bank did not ask Lao PDR to bypass any existing institutions. Rather, it focused on strengthening the country's existing institutional structure and the processes and incentive systems that underlie it to make them more transparent and accountable. The NGPES was produced by the government and based on extensive consultations. The World Bank and the government also painstakingly negotiated the public finance management reform program. Recognizing that the government would not accept any route it perceived as inconsistent with its sovereignty, the Bank team built on country ownership throughout the process.

Other development partners also supported the NGPES. ADB provided technical assistance for public expenditure management and, particularly, for the development of a medium-term fiscal framework, which advisers on the ground helped implement. The IMF also supported the fiscal and macroeconomic strategy. Its own reform program, the Poverty Reduction and Growth Facility (PRGF), had gone off track in early 2005, largely because of slow progress in strengthening tax policy and tax and customs administration, the failure to reach agreement on an independent audit of the central bank, and the approval by the National Assembly of a 2004/05 budget that the IMF viewed as unrealistic and excessively expansionary. Despite that experience, the IMF provided letters to the World Bank and ADB boards that supported the broad macroeconomic performance of Lao PDR, while highlighting remaining risks and structural weaknesses.

The government proved able to manage the challenges to macroeconomic stability better than some had anticipated. Large budgeted wage increases were stretched out over time. Tax revenues, which had softened as logging royalties declined, picked up, with mineral royalties playing an important role. The budget deficit was contained, inflation gradually declined, exports grew, and GDP growth steadily exceeded 6 percent a year. Significant foreign direct investment from China, Thailand, and Vietnam financed the current account deficit, allowing foreign exchange reserves to steadily increase. Unlike other low-income countries, Lao PDR was able to avoid defaulting on its external debt (although it qualified for debt relief under the Multilateral Debt Relief Initiative). In forgoing such assistance, the government sent a signal about its seriousness in honoring foreign commitments. At the same time, it embarked on a process of renegotiating its Soviet-era debt to reflect more realistic exchange rates and the new relationship with the Russian Federation. Total debt service fell below 10 percent of government revenue and to 7 percent of exports in 2006. None of the adverse macroeconomic concerns related to exchange rate appreciation, Dutch disease, or overheating came to pass.

The Revenue and Expenditure Management Framework

The principal development benefits of NT2 are the royalties, dividends, and taxes the Nam Theun 2 Power Company pays to the national treasury. Realizing these benefits required an improved revenue and expenditure management framework. The NT2 project rested on four pillars of revenue management: the allocation of budget resources, the flow of funds, reporting, and the monitoring and evaluation of effectiveness. Each of these areas was contentious.

An approach was needed that would be acceptable to the World Bank as well as to the government. The government was unwilling to accept more than minimal intrusion in the management of its public finances and viewed the resources from NT2 as sovereign. Moreover, the central government lacked complete control over the budget, because local governments have extensive powers over tax collection and spending and can sometimes circumvent national edicts. This complicated the policy debate over eligible programs for poverty reduction from NT2 revenues and the establishment of baseline figures for judging how incremental revenues should be spent.

The government and the World Bank also differed on the flow of funds arrangements. The Bank was keen to develop a mechanism that guaranteed that NT2 resources would be used for their designated poverty reduction purposes. In an environment in which the state audit organization was weak; the IMF program had already gone off track, partly because of a deadlock over the independent audit of the Bank of Lao PDR; and the budget was opaque, the World Bank needed a mechanism to demonstrate clearly how the revenues from NT2 would be spent. In other countries, the Bank had supported revenue-management arrangements that earmarked specific revenue shares for poverty projects, along with independent oversight to monitor the use of revenues.[2] The government of Lao PDR, however, emphasized that any proposal including a third-country escrow of NT2 revenues or a tap beyond the control of the Ministry of Finance would not be acceptable.

The government's proposal was to strengthen its existing systems through an improved public financial management system with appropriate transparency and accountability rather than earmarking and tracking specific NT2 resources. Because of the failure of previous efforts by the donor community to strengthen the government's public finance management, World Bank staff had strong doubts that the overall public finance management system could be made transparent and accountable enough within five years. Given the slow pace of any kind of reform in Lao PDR, it seemed unlikely that an accelerated approach would work. A compromise two-track approach to reforming public finance management was therefore agreed upon, in which one track focused on overall systems strengthening and the other provided specific NT2 revenue management arrangements as a fallback to be used if the overall system did not meet certain performance thresholds.

Track One sought to improve the transparency, management, and accountability of government resources. These improvements were spelled out in the PEMSP, an ambitious effort for a country with limited domestic capacity. The PEMSP is comprehensive and includes programs to improve fiscal planning and budget preparation, Treasury functions, accounting and reporting, information systems, and the legislative framework for public expenditure management. A sequence of PRSOs, conducted since 2005, has supported and monitored progress on this program. The FMCBC financed technical assistance.

The danger in such a comprehensive program is that the government—and support from the donor community—will be stretched too thin. Some government officials expressed the view that the PEMSP should be seen as a generic document that needs to be tailored to the Lao environment, focused, and prioritized. Successful implementation of even a refocused program, however, will require critical improvements in government capacity.

Track Two established specific revenue-management arrangements for NT2 revenues, which are a small fraction (less than 10 percent) of overall government resources. These arrangements consist of the identification of priority programs based on the National Socio-Economic Development Plan (NSEDP, the successor to the NGPES): for example, in basic education, basic health, rural roads, and specific poverty reduction and environmental conservation projects. Track Two also specifies a mechanism for ensuring that NT2 resources for these priority programs are additional to other budget resources. It calls for channeling revenues through an NT2 subaccount at the Treasury that can be audited separately from the overall Treasury account. It provides for the publication of budget execution reports, financial statements, and summaries of internal audit reports and audits of eligible programs and for the implementation of public expenditure tracking surveys and public expenditure reviews to assess the control environment and the impact of incremental expenditures on program performance and poverty reduction outcomes.

If Track One results in an acceptable level of soundness in the overall public finance management system by the time NT2 revenues begin flowing, specific revenue management measures will become redundant. This potential redundancy of Track Two was strategically embedded in the revenue-management options to create an incentive for the government to deliver on overall systems strengthening. At the same time, the combination of the two tracks provided comfort within the World Bank that, in either case, NT2 revenues would be transparently and judiciously used for their intended poverty reduction purposes.

Reaching Consensus: The Decision Framework and Its Implementation

Embedding NT2 in a comprehensive program exposed the project to a number of risks: a bottleneck anywhere in the web of arrangements could delay the project. For that reason, it was critical to define a set of principles early on that would explicitly lay out the parameters under which World Bank support for the project would be forthcoming. The Bank had to balance support of the project against insistence that this support remain conditional on progress on several key issues. If the Bank had committed to support the project too early, it would have missed the opportunity to also support the broad development agenda that was required to yield the poverty reduction impact. If it asked too much, the government would not have been able to deliver and might have tried to develop the project with other partners.

Beginning in August 2001, the government and the World Bank operated within an agreed decision framework, which was made public in July 2002 (see chapter 1). It stipulated that project processing would be linked, among other things, to the government's progress in implementing a development framework with concrete performance on poverty reduction and environmental protection. The development framework included a poverty reduction strategy and implementation plan; a public financial management system, featuring audit and accountability as well as transparency and disclosure mechanisms; sector policies and regulation in regard to private sector participation; and safeguard policies and standards. The framework recognized that the development impact of NT2 would be determined by the extent to which the policy and institutional framework in place would ensure effective use of the revenues generated by the project. It also recognized that mobilization of broad support for the project among key stakeholders in Lao PDR and abroad would be critical if NT2 was to play a constructive role as a driver of reform. The decision framework helped the Bank reach agreement with the government on the broad principles to be followed and the expected outcomes. It did so in a nonmechanistic manner that left room for judgment and midcourse correction.

In balancing flexibility with ex ante transparent conditions, the NT2 process required a new approach by the World Bank. This approach called for a very high degree of due diligence; a high level of management involvement and a consensus-building approach within and outside the Bank (to frame judgments on adequacy of progress); a dedicated team that could be empowered to develop solutions on the ground; and dialogue and partnerships with government and other project stakeholders characterized by respect, openness, consistency, and perseverance over a broad array of topics.

Such a process is easier to describe than to implement. In practice, the decision framework provided room for judgment, and there was ambiguity regarding exactly what the deal-breakers were. This left the Lao PDR government with considerable uncertainty and a sense of "moving targets" that made it hard for it to plan and execute. On the World Bank side, greater specificity was not feasible, because management was not sure what would be required to ensure stakeholders inside and outside the institution would fully support moving ahead.

The process of building consensus was based on a vast and solid foundation of analytical work. The diagnostics included, but were not limited to, a country economic memorandum, a financial and economic analysis, a macroeconomic analysis, a social and environmental impact assessment, a public expenditure review, a country financial accountability assessment, and the decision framework. The country economic memorandum, which was initiated when the World Bank reengaged in NT2 in 2001, was of particular importance. It aimed at detailing the broad development options for Lao PDR. It stressed that hydropower was the only obvious comparative advantage of Lao PDR and that hydropower development was crucial to achieving the growth targets articulated in the NGPES—a point that country economic memorandums had consistently made since 1979. It also pointed out the broad changes in economic management required to translate hydropower development into sustainable growth and poverty reduction.

Building consensus required time. Based on past performance, there was skepticism within the World Bank and among external stakeholders about the willingness and ability of the government to continue moving ahead with pro-market reforms. For its part, the government had doubts about the World Bank's readiness to support the project without insisting on a range of overly intrusive conditions. A confidence- and credibility-building process was put in place involving specification of time-bound reform targets and monitoring of implementation over the 2002–05 period (this process remains in place today). The major elements of this process were contained in the FMAC, which was disbursed in two tranches, an unusual procedure for the World Bank at the time. The first tranche was disbursed upon effectiveness of the credit, based on actions undertaken by 2002. The second tranche required the government to maintain a satisfactory macroeconomic policy framework and to meet 17 milestones in the reform of the public sector and, crucially, state enterprises and state-owned banks. The reforms included some politically problematic measures, such as restructuring powerful state enterprises, slashing subsidies, and raising utility tariffs to achieve cost recovery. They also dealt with the difficult issue of nonperforming loans at state banks.

It took the government a year longer than expected to meet the reform targets, but every action was completed before disbursement of the second tranche in mid-2004. To the surprise of many, the government did not ask for any waivers. It completed the program in full, sending a strong signal about its willingness and ability to design and implement a broad-based reform strategy. This initial program was succeeded by a series of PRSOs that pushed the reform agenda forward on an annual basis.

During the course of implementation of the reform program, it was apparent that significant support for capacity building would be required. Building capacity is a formidable task in any country; it is particularly challenging when a country has limited experience with practices across the world. Opportunities to get started early in the process were lost because of uncertainty regarding eventual World Bank support for NT2 and government concerns about borrowing for training and technical assistance.

The country team enlisted the support of the World Bank Institute in carrying out a capacity-building needs assessment. That assessment formed the basis of a country assistance strategy in which capacity building featured prominently. The World Bank and the government agreed early on to an FMCBC, but the government was not happy about using scarce IDA credits for such purposes, preferring to fund capacity building with grants. Because Lao PDR had limited access to grants, the World Bank tried to enlist the financial support of other development partners, without much success. In 2005 implementation of the PEMSP had just begun and public finance management capacity-building lagged. Because PEMSP is funded through limited government resources, with only a few advisers provided through official development assistance, mobilizing financial and technical support to bring capacity to the needed levels to deliver a sound public finance management system by the time NT2 revenues started to flow required Herculean efforts. To make matters worse, the IMF program went off track in 2005, when negotiations on the Russian debt appeared to have concluded on terms perceived as favorable to Russian creditors,[3] public sector wage increases threatened the budget, and efforts to sell the loss-making national airline fell apart, exposing the government to major losses.

Before they presented NT2 to the Board, World Bank managers had to determine whether each of these developments could derail achievement of project objectives within the planned timeline (and therefore required urgent attention and action) or could be mitigated through further dialogue and reform. These matters were discussed at project oversight group meetings chaired by the regional vice president or his deputy that included all relevant sector directors, the country director, and other senior managers. Discussion of controversial issues such as the IMF program, revenue management, and social and environmental assessment continued until consensus was reached on the proposed approach. The process was time consuming, but it helped the team make better decisions. Once decisions were made, the whole team owned the outcome and any remaining internal disagreements were shelved. Most important, since government ownership was respected, decisions were in line with the government's strategy.

Lessons Learned

Many lessons emerge from the preparation of NT2. They include lessons on establishing the development framework, building trust with government and other stakeholders, and gearing the World Bank internally to deliver.

Establishing the Development Framework

To provide NT2 with the foundation needed to achieve the desired development objectives, the government needed to demonstrate progress on a range of policy and institutional reforms supporting improved public finance management, poverty reduction, and environmental protection, as laid out in the decision framework. Specific recommendations based on the World Bank's experience with NT2 are described below.

Embed the project in the national poverty reduction strategy, and use Development Policy Loans (DPLs) as implementation and monitoring tools. Thorough integration of NT2 into a poverty-focused national development strategy provided the poverty reduction orientation needed for the World Bank's and other partners' involvement. This was a departure from the usual way in which the World Bank views large infrastructure projects in difficult environments. The engagement strategy to support the poverty reduction framework was clear from the beginning and well articulated in the country assistance strategy and implemented chiefly through DPLs. By focusing the overall assistance strategy on reforms and capacity building, the country assistance strategy allowed the NT2 project team to focus on the project itself while others on the country team focused on overall development issues. Using DPLs as the key vehicle for spelling out and monitoring key reforms allowed for an ongoing country dialogue on critical issues.

Conduct comprehensive and integrated diagnostic work. The diagnostic work to support the strategy and its various components was comprehensive in scope and carried out in an integrated manner. Analytical work was important to ensure that policy choices were based on solid technical analysis and shared between partners rather than based on negotiations between adversaries. Analytical work also provided the channel for communicating findings to the broad array of stakeholders in the project. Although many stakeholders complained about the extensiveness of analytical work ("we don't need more studies"), the content of the reports and the process of engaging with government officials in a policy dialogue on the basis of analytical work were critical to building understanding.

Judge the government's commitment and capacity to deliver on policy reform and poverty reduction on the basis of its track record—and be willing to walk away. Lao PDR had a reasonable record of poverty reduction before the project, but an uneven record on economic reform. Without further reforms, the core poverty reduction impact of the project would be at risk. The judgment about reforms was therefore central to the justification for World Bank engagement, not simply a way of taking advantage of the leverage offered by Bank financial support for the project. Judgments had to be made based on outcomes as well as intermediate policy actions requiring significant political commitment for implementation.[4] Crucially, these judgments were seen as make-or-break milestones for the project.

It was important for the World Bank and other partners to accept that they could not turn around lack of political will with NT2 project design and the introduction of new institutions. The Bank could not commit to support the project before a policy track record was established. The Bank also had to be willing to walk away from support to the project if critical conditions were not fulfilled. The Bank's willingness to walk away is particularly important in projects generating substantial government revenue, because in the hands of rent-seeking governments, such projects can help precipitate a resource curse that weakens governance and development outcomes and increases the chances of conflict.

Leave room for flexibility and support government ownership. The decision-making framework focused on principles of engagement and the attainment of specific objectives, not specific policies. As the track record of the government improved, its ownership of the reform program became systematically stronger. The FMAC was seen as a process that imposed conditions from outside Lao PDR. In contrast, the successor PRSOs are now seen differently. Flexibility and a step-by-step approach to conditionality, rather than a focus on a few headline reform items, were key to this change in perception and the ensuing sustainability of the overall reform program. That foundation is more critical to overall success than any one individual policy reform. Flexibility was especially critical in designing Track Two, in managing the Russian debt issue, and in overcoming the failure of the IMF reform program.

Build on country processes and systems. NT2 and the broader development strategy were built on strengthened country systems and processes. The NGPES and its successor, the NSEDP, aimed to make government processes and policies more open and transparent, more tightly focused on poverty reduction, and more oriented toward the achievement of specific development results. The same was true of the public finance management reform program. Rather than trying to bypass government institutions and systems, the World Bank and other partners focused on strengthening existing ones, even when implementation was difficult because of limited domestic capacity.

Identify critical areas of weak capacity early on, and design a capacity-building strategy to address them. More could have been done in this area. The World Bank toolkit and professional and financial resources for effectively supporting capacity building could have been mobilized more effectively, and in the absence of a Bank commitment early enough to support the project, the government's response to suggested capacity-building activities was at best lukewarm.

Take the time to prepare the groundwork properly. From a project point of view, and from the perspective of many stakeholders, too much time was taken to prepare NT2, and the process of deliberations before the World Bank committed to providing financial support was too drawn out. From the perspective of Lao PDR getting ready for NT2, however, the elapsed time period may have been too short. Lao PDR's track record of reform had to be built in about the same time frame as that considered the minimum for countries receiving debt relief. Implementing major elements of the public financial management program would take years. Indeed, cross-country experience suggests that 10 years is a reasonable period of time in which to reform budget systems, adopt a new control system, and develop and implement a chart of accounts.

Building Trust with Government and Other Stakeholders

Developing trust among partners is important in all infrastructure projects. It was particularly important in NT2, because of the project's high visibility, large size, and complexity; the political, social and economic context in which it was implemented; and the large number and wide variety of project stakeholders. Developing trust and fostering stakeholder partnerships were essential to working through constraints and competing needs to achieve common objectives. Specific recommendations based on the World Bank's experience with NT2 are described below.

Understand the country's political and cultural context, including its formal and informal rules, in order to elicit the government's trust. The World Bank's team had some understanding of and sensitivity to the political and cultural context in Lao PDR, which helped it devise the right engagement strategy and behave in an appropriate manner. This was particularly important in the lengthy and at times frustrating process of negotiation. Lao PDR's decisions were made in an opaque manner that was little understood by the World Bank. Unseen factors, such as personal links among the elite, party affiliations, and wartime histories, provided as much authority to individuals in the government as their formal positions. This meant that government negotiating teams were not fully empowered to make decisions on the spot but had to conduct time-consuming internal consultations in order to build consensus within the government and obtain the approval of the officials with the real power to make decisions. Sensitivity to these conditions was a critical ingredient in the eventual development of a relationship of mutual trust with the government.

Engage the government early on with an open mind, and support reformers. Government ownership is critical to success. The World Bank should not wait until its position is fully fleshed out to engage with the government. Rather, it should view its decision-making process as a joint and dynamic process of analysis and engagement by the World Bank, the government, and any other stakeholders. It is useful to approach the Bank's relationship with the government as a joint learning exercise and, hence, to be ready to learn from the government in order to maximize Bank effectiveness and to take the time to encourage learning by the Bank's counterparts. In particular, the World Bank should support reformers in the manner that is most appropriate in each country's context. This process helps buttress project success and contributes to the sustainability of reform.

Encourage openness, respect, and consistency, all of which are critical ingredients to the development of trust. The team took pains to try to be clear and consistent in its articulation of the World Bank's positions, particularly in distinguishing deal-breaker issues from other issues. Making clear what was required of the government for the project to go ahead was critical to saving time and building trust. Within the World Bank, the team spelled out progress on other challenges (non–deal breakers), so that the seriousness and urgency of the issues was conveyed appropriately to senior management.

Gain support from other stakeholders. Regarding country economic elements, the World Bank's two most important official partners were the ADB and the IMF. Through its long history of engagement with public finance management reform in Lao PDR, the ADB had developed a relationship of trust that allowed it to bridge the gap between the positions of the government and the World Bank. ADB support for the project became critical for its eventual success.

In contrast, the IMF had issues with the government over the reform program that it was unable to resolve. Although the World Bank has traditionally been very reluctant to move forward with reform operations without a formal IMF program in place, doing so was necessary and manageable in this instance. Implicit IMF support, in the form of a letter of support on the macroeconomic program and the inclusion of compensatory macroeconomic monitoring indicators in the World Bank program, sufficed.

Gearing the World Bank Internally to Deliver

Building and maintaining effective internal team and management relationships and tapping flexibility and creativity to overcome obstacles were critical to managing institutional risks and delivering on heavy project preparation demands. Specific recommendations based on the World Bank's experience with NT2 are described below.

Select a broad-based management team. Making the project into a regional priority—with shared responsibilities among a number of directors, under the oversight of the regional vice president—ensured widespread ownership. Three sector directors and the country director had de facto veto power, as each had deal-breaker issues within his areas of responsibility. Although some argued that a single director should take charge of all aspects of the project, doing so might have undermined the scope of support that was mobilized. Moreover, no single director had the technical experience to oversee all facets of what became a comprehensive, integrated set of development projects.

Engage management at the highest level of the World Bank early on, and gain its explicit support. NT2 was a very high-profile project (French president Jacques Chirac, for example, wrote a letter of support for the project at a critical juncture). Civil society organizations from around the world focused on how the project evolved. The Bank's president was eager to ensure that support be as widespread as possible among responsible groups.

Judicious intervention by the World Bank president and managing director at specific points in the process was crucial: government officials report that they were convinced of Bank support when the managing director visited the country, even though negotiations were still ongoing at that point. The later visit of the World Bank's president and his intervention when the major project developer temporarily withdrew (for political reasons) helped seal the deal. These interventions were possible only because senior management was fully aware of project progress and lent its support to the decision framework.

Do not take World Bank precedents as given; take some risks. The NT2 development process shows that flexibility and creativity in working within World Bank rules can deliver for the project and the client country as well as for the Bank. As Lao PDR prepared for NT2, some contentious issues called for solutions that departed from World Bank norms. For example, PRSCs and PRSOs are not recommended for countries with low CPIA scores or no formal IMF programs. In this case, however, they were needed to build a track record of reform. The approach to public financial management had to be based on a set of initial reforms that pertained to the local situation. The Track One/Track Two arrangements satisfied neither the "purists," who were insistent on the primacy of strengthening country systems, nor the "realists," who pushed for an external control mechanism. The focus of financial sector reforms was on containment of nonperforming loans, not on privatization. In each of these areas, the NT2 team had to depart from World Bank orthodoxy and the recommendations of network sector specialists in order to tailor the program to Lao PDR development needs and political realities.

Accept that developing a good project with a systemic approach takes time, resources, and commitment. This is particularly true when the project and the country context are complex. The World Bank needed time to carry out due diligence properly, including through high-quality diagnostic work; the government needed time to deliver on its reform agenda. Time was also needed to build trust among stakeholders, in particular between the World Bank and the government, and to strengthen the hands of reformers, increasing the chances of project and reform success. The project costs far exceeded normal World Bank levels; preparation was possible only because regional management provided resources up front, and negotiated a significant fee with the project developers (realized ex post). Formal and informal commitments, captured in a range of instruments and modalities between various partners, were also essential to ensuring that common objectives were met and the high level of resources and time expended to accomplish those objectives sustained.

Notes

1. The World Bank's CPIA assesses the quality of a country's policy and institutional framework in fostering sustainable growth, poverty reduction, and the effective use of development assistance. Governance Matters IV presents updated aggregate governance indicators (covering 209 countries over the period 1996–2004) and analyzes issues related to the use of the measures.
2. In Chad, for example, a formally independent Collège de Controle et de Surveillance des Ressources Petrolières was created to monitor revenues from the Chad-Cameroon pipeline project.
3. The terms the government agreed to were especially unfavorable compared with the discounts received by Mongolia at about this time. The Lao PDR negotiations were held in secret, and the terms were not transparent, as they included barter agreements (with unclear prices) as part of the package.
4. In the short run, the areas that are most clearly within a government's control and hence responsibility are inputs (financial and policy inputs) and outputs (for example, schools built, health workers deployed, institutions built). In the medium run, the government also plays a critical role in affecting intermediate indicators (for example, school enrollment rates, the number of outpatient visits to a clinic). In the long run, governments are also a critical determinant of final outcomes (for example, economic growth, literacy, infant mortality rates).

CHAPTER 3

The Project Is Prepared

Teresa Serra, Mark Segal, and Ram Chopra

The second element of the decision framework for the Nam Theun 2 (NT2) project focused on ensuring that the technical/engineering, financial, and economic aspects of the project and the design and implementation of environmental and social safeguard programs were of a standard acceptable to the World Bank. These aspects of the project were the subject of intense due diligence during project preparation.

The hydropower aspects of the project benefited from the experience of the developers. The Dam Safety Review Panel, made up of internationally recognized experts on the design, construction, and operation of hydropower projects, was heavily involved throughout the design process. Designs prepared by internationally reputable firms were fine-tuned based on advice from and recommendations by the panel and reviewed by World Bank experts. This process provided the necessary degree of assurance that NT2 conformed to best international practices in terms of technical design. Project procurement was also studied in depth to ensure that it met the World Bank's economy and efficiency guidelines for guarantee operations and that project costs were reasonable.

Teresa Serra prepared the section on environmental and social safeguards, with assistance from Bruce Harris and Tom Walton. Mark Segal prepared the section on project economic analysis. Ram Chopra prepared the section on the financial package for NT2. In addition, the contributions of Christian Delvoie, Suman Babbar, Pankaj Gupta, Robert Mertz, Glenn Morgan, Chaohua Zhang, Anthony Whitten, Svend Jensby, and Ron Zweig are gratefully acknowledged.

51

In addition to the technical/engineering aspects of the project, the social and environmental issues, project economic analysis, and the financial package for NT2 received due diligence during project preparation; and it is these issues that are the focus of this chapter.

Social and Environmental Issues

NT2 presented a unique opportunity for refining the World Bank's approach to environmental and social safeguards in large infrastructure operations with widespread regional and cumulative impacts. Impact assessment and mitigation planning therefore had to be comprehensive in scope and faced five important challenges:

- Managing environmental and social impacts spread over six zones: the Nakai plateau (where the reservoir would be formed); the NT2 watershed (comprising the Nakai Nam Theun National Protected Area and two corridors linking it to other national protected areas); the downstream areas of the Nam Theun and Xe Bang Fai basins; other project-impacted lands (needed for construction camps, quarries, roads and transmission lines); and the Mekong River (with transboundary implications).
- Resettlement of about 6,200 people living on the plateau, of which the most seriously affected were ethnic minority villagers with limited ability to cope with displacement and changes in livelihood patterns.
- Impacts on the livelihoods of watershed and downstream households, totaling some 70,000 people, which, though not displaced, were also affected in varying degrees by the project and, in many cases, required adequate support to transition to alternative productive activities.
- Uncertainty affecting project impacts in some cases, which meant that decision making and mitigation planning had to rely on the use of adaptive approaches and contingency measures to address unanticipated impacts.
- Numerous operational/institutional opportunities and constraints posed by the public-private nature of NT2, requiring that appropriate balance be found with regard to the pursuit of project efficiency, regional development, and national capacity building, in the short and longer term.

World Bank Safeguard Policies and Sectoral Best Practice

The project triggered all 10 of the World Bank's safeguards policies (box 3.1). The Bank faced several challenges in applying these policies and in promoting

Box 3.1
The World Bank's Environmental and Social Safeguard Policies

The World Bank's environmental and social safeguard policies are a cornerstone of its support to sustainable poverty reduction. The objective of these 10 policies is to prevent and mitigate undue harm to people and their environment in the development process. The policies provide guidelines for World Bank and borrower staffs in identifying, preparing, and implementing programs and projects in the following areas:

- Environmental Assessment (Operational Policy [OP]) 4.01) is the World Bank's umbrella policy used to identify, avoid, and mitigate the potential negative impacts associated with Bank investment operations, with the purpose of improving decision making while ensuring that project options under consideration are sound and sustainable and that potentially affected people have been properly consulted.
- Involuntary Resettlement (OP 4.12): Involuntary resettlement should be avoidable or minimized where feasible. Where displacement is unavoidable, resettlement plans should be developed and executed as development programs with the objective to ensure that the population displaced by a project benefits from the project including: affected persons consultation and participation in planning and implementing resettlement to improve their livelihoods and standards of living, at least restoring them to predisplacement levels, in real terms.
- Indigenous Peoples (Operational Directive [OD] 4.20): In force and applicable during NT2 Project processing, the objectives of this policy are: (i) to ensure that Indigenous Peoples benefit from development projects, and (ii) avoid or mitigate potentially adverse effects on Indigenous Peoples caused by Bank-financed or assisted activities. The policy requires special action where Bank investments affect Indigenous Peoples.
- Natural Habitats (OP 4.04): The Bank does not support projects that involve the significant conversion of critical natural habitat. Bank-financed projects are sited on land already converted when feasible. If noncritical natural habitats would be significantly converted, acceptable mitigation measures are included in project design including obligation to take into account the views and roles of affected groups (NGOs, communities) in project design/implementation, minimizing habitat loss, and establishing and maintaining ecologically similar protected areas with adequate institutional capacity of the implementing organization.
- Pest Management (OP 4.09): The Bank supports controlling pests primarily through environmental methods and/or control of disease vectors. Pesticide uses are assessed in the context of the project's environmental assessment against the following criteria, among others: they must have (i) negligible adverse health effects, and (ii) minimal effect on nontarget species and environment.

(Box continues on the following page.)

Box 3.1 (*continued*)

- Cultural Property (Operational Policy Note [OPN] 11.03): In force and applicable during NT2 Project processing, the Bank's general policy is to assist in preservation and to avoid elimination of cultural properties. More specifically, the objectives of the OPN are: (i) to avoid any significant damage to nonreplicable cultural property, (ii) assist only those projects that are sited or designed so as to prevent such damage, and (iii) assist in the protection and enhancement of cultural properties encountered in Bank-financed projects.
- Forests (OP 4.36): The objective of this policy is to assist borrowers to harness the potential of the forest to reduce poverty in a sustainable manner, integrate forests effectively into sustainable economic development, and protect the vital local and global environmental services and values of forests. The Bank does not finance projects that would involve significant conversion or degradation of critical forest areas or related critical natural habitats.
- Safety of Dams (OP 4.37) requires the technical review of designs by independent dam safety professionals and calls on the borrower to adopt and implement dam safety measures throughout the project cycle.
- Projects on International Waterways (OP 7.50) requires that the proposed project not affect the efficient utilization and protection of international waterways. It requires the borrower to notify the other riparian of the proposed project and its details. Riparian are expected, within the existing legal arrangements for the international waterways, where they are in place or otherwise, to provide their views on the proposed project to the borrower, which will inform the Bank accordingly. The World Bank may appoint a panel of experts to review any objection from riparian before deciding on financing the proposed project.
- Projects in Disputed Areas (OP 7.60) requires the World Bank, early in the project processing cycle, to ensure that countries involved in a dispute over an area where a proposed project is to be implemented have no objection to the proposed project.

Public consultation is required for the first seven of these policies. In addition, the World Bank requires public disclosure of information about proposed projects and their impacts, in English and local languages, at its public information centers and at project sites, or at sites that are easily accessible to interested parties.

the adoption of sectoral best practice. The Lao government, the Nam Theun 2 Power Company (NTPC), and other stakeholders saw the World Bank as continuously expanding both the geographical scope and the thematic coverage of the studies called for. The developer claimed that, by increasing demands for environmental and social analyses, the World Bank was "shifting goalposts" without clearly defining an acceptable set of requirements. In contrast, tensions also arose because other (usually external) stakeholders believed that the environmental and social analyses were not sufficiently comprehensive, and that some critical potential problems or groups of people who would be affected by the project were ignored. Different stakeholders' expectations and challenges came to the fore in the drafting and revisions of the documentation required to address the environmental and social aspects of the project, including the Environmental Assessment and Management Plan (EAMP), the Social Development Plan (SDP), and the Social and Environment Management Framework and First Operational Plan (SEMFOP) for the Nam Theun watershed.

Project Impact Zones

The adverse social and environmental impacts of the NT2 project resulted from impoundment of the Nam Theun River to form a 450-square-kilometer seasonally variable reservoir; the interbasin transfer of water from the Nam Theun River to the Xe Bang Fai River, with associated changes in flow patterns and aquatic ecology; and the construction of project ancillary works. This section looks at the impacts on each of the six areas affected by the project.

The Nakai plateau. About 60 percent of the Nakai plateau was covered by forest of variable quality, ranging from undisturbed to highly disturbed. A natural habitats accounting assessment identified the forest types that would be lost to inundation. Although this area had been under pressure for many years, it still contained animal species that were important from a conservation perspective, including the Asian elephant, the white-winged duck, and several other bird species. There were significant tracts of contiguous forest area, especially on the northeast side of the plateau, near the dam.

The major environmental impacts of the project on the plateau related to natural habitat loss and its implications for wildlife conservation. The EAMP called for this loss (along with impacts on natural habitats in other project-affected areas) to be mitigated and compensated through direct interventions, such as wildlife and reservoir management programs on the plateau, as well as by protection of the NT2 watershed. In addition, the EAMP included financial support for surveys, species-focused programs, and environmental education.

The communities on the Nakai plateau included five main ethnolinguistic groups: Brou (40 percent), Tai Bo (40 percent), Upland Tai (11 percent), Vietic (6 percent), and Sek (1 percent). The communities were dependent on *swidden* (shifting cultivation) farming, hunting and gathering of timber and nontimber forest products, fishing, livestock, and wage income. Only 17 percent of the families could produce sufficient rice for the year, and 50 percent suffered rice deficiency during more than six months per year. Average household income (both cash and imputed) was $450 per year, well below the national poverty line of $800 per year. Agricultural production was constrained by poor soils, adverse weather conditions, lack of modern farming techniques, and lack of access to markets. Most households had no electricity, access to clean water was limited, and paved roads were unavailable. Social conditions were similarly precarious: more than 60 percent of the population had no schooling, and the average distance to the nearest health facility was 11 kilometers, usually traveled on foot.

The project required the relocation of about 17 villages, comprising about 6,200 people, predominantly ethnic minorities. The Resettlement Action Plan (RAP) detailed in the SDP, developed with the participation of the affected population, aimed to improve the lives of displaced villagers through livelihoods programs that included community forestry, reservoir fisheries, household gardens, irrigated rice farming, and livestock husbandry. NTPC committed to raising the average income of resettler households, by the start of year 5 after relocation, to the greater of the then national poverty line or an alternative income threshold equivalent to $800 (at June 2002 values). Both the government and NTPC also committed to an ambitious "best endeavor" target, by year 9 after relocation, of raising the average income of villages in the NT2 resettlement area to the greater of the then national average rural income level or an alternative threshold equivalent of $1,200 (at June 2002 values).

In addition to the livelihoods programs, the RAP provided land, housing, infrastructure (for example, water supply, sanitation, electricity, roads), and social services (for example, health and education). It also included measures to assist ethnic minorities and other especially vulnerable households in culturally appropriate ways (box 3.2). Measures were incorporated to address numerous specific concerns (for example, that the demand for the output of the newly introduced crops would be limited or that the rotting of biomass in the flooded area could severely reduce fish populations). The relocation and livelihoods programs were frontloaded to allow opportunity to assess the

---

Box 3.2
Addressing Gender Issues

Addressing gender issues was an integral part of the NT2 project design. A gender assessment found that women and girls, particularly those from certain marginalized ethnic groups and those living within disadvantaged households, had limited access to education, off-farm employment, production markets, cash assets, and sociopolitical empowerment. The assessment concluded that these groups faced greater risks in the resettlement process and would require continual and intense attention and support.

A Gender Strategy and Action Plan was developed and incorporated within the SDP. Actions included identification of gender-specific impacts and issues; gender-sensitive and participatory planning, monitoring, and mitigation mechanisms; promotion of gender-balanced community institutions; gender-sensitive opportunities for income generation and skills development, training, and off-farm work opportunities; and community education on alcoholism, spouse abuse, and sexually transmitted infections, including HIV.

---

adaptation of the resettled people to new conditions and to adjust the programs as needed early on.

The Nam Theun watershed. The NT2 watershed, comprising the Nakai Nam Theun National Protected Area and two adjoining corridors, is an area of national and international importance for biodiversity. It is known for the quality and diversity of ecological habitats, which includes populations of many rare, endangered, and vulnerable species. Because the watershed is contiguous with areas of international conservation status on the Vietnamese side of the border, it presented both important opportunities and challenges.

Conservation in Lao PDR has suffered from a range of problems, including insufficient funding, weak technical capacity, and limited emphasis on enforcement. Indicative of the conservation challenge is the fact that during the 1990s, commercial logging took place in the Nakai plateau, at times extending into the national protected area. Preparation of the NT2 project caused the government to enforce a logging ban in the area. As an offset for biodiversity losses on the plateau and other project lands, the NT2 project established a watershed conservation program to be implemented by the government and to which NTPC will be providing $31.5 million over a 30-year period.

About 5,800 people—90 percent of them members of indigenous Brou, Phong, Kri, and Sek groups—lived in 35 villages within the Nam Theun watershed. In addition, the peripheral impact zone adjacent to the watershed (north, south, and west of the protected area) consisted of 54 villages with a total estimated population of about 22,500 and household income levels well below the national poverty line. Most villages practiced shifting cultivation and collected nontimber forest products, including wildlife. They had limited access to infrastructure and social services, including health care.

The NT2 project would not displace these populations, but conservation plans for the watershed would limit their access to natural resources. Communities and individuals would be adversely affected by improved enforcement of existing regulations, such as those concerning wildlife hunting, as well as by the introduction of new land and resource use patterns that in some cases could impose spatial and temporal resource access restrictions.

Under the SEMFOP, protection and conservation objectives were reconciled with the development aspirations of watershed populations, ensuring that they benefited from and supported the program. It was foreseen that they would ultimately benefit from enhanced land and resource use rights, improved livelihoods through natural resource management activities, and improved access to basic services such as water supply and sanitation, health facilities, and schools. Natural resource use arrangements would be agreed upon with the affected villages, and adverse impacts would be compensated for through livelihood and community development activities. Measures would be taken to address these issues through a participatory village planning process involving all groups.

The Xe Bang Fai basin. The Xe Bang Fai provided water for irrigation, fishing, and household use to some 100,000 people. The water quality was good, with adequate dissolved oxygen and low levels of turbidity. After the start of commercial operation, NT2 was expected to have a significant impact on aquatic habitats and fisheries through flow changes (including doubling the average annual flow and changing the variability in weekly and seasonal flows), increased erosion, and changes in water quality. In addition, the potential for flooding would increase. Measures to reduce these impacts included specially designed aeration structures and a regulating pond. To prevent poor water quality and manage extreme variations in water flows, the EAMP called for biomass reduction on the plateau before filling the reservoir; intake of water from the reservoir allowing a mix of low and high levels of dissolved oxygen; and operating rules that would reduce (or stop) generation during periods of inundation of the Xe Bang Fai floodplain.

Before NT2, the communities in the Xe Bang Fai floodplain were largely dependent on paddy rice cultivation, livestock rearing, fishing, and wage income. Average household income was about $660 per year, and although noticeably better off than plateau and watershed residents, about 40 percent of the population lived below the national poverty line. Most of the population was from the Lao ethnic group, but the communities also included ethnic minorities (mostly Brou).

As a result of changes in the siting of the downstream channel, resettlement of households along the Xe Bang Fai was avoided. However, after the start of commercial operations, the changes in the river's flow regime and water quality, noted above, will reduce the productivity of fisheries and inundate physical assets, such as water supply systems, irrigation pumps, river crossings, riverbank gardens, and other productive lands. These changes could directly affect as many as 40,000 people on the main course of the Xe Bang Fai (with the impacts becoming milder toward the confluence with the Mekong); another 30,000 people living near or along tributaries to the Xe Bang Fai could also be adversely affected to varying degrees, through reduced access to river fisheries.

In addition to the measures foreseen in the EAMP, the SDP included provisions for asset replacement and restoration of livelihoods, developed in consultation with potentially affected communities. River bank protection and the possible construction of dikes in the lower segment of the river were also foreseen. Baselines for fish productivity and catch were established, and alternative models for restoration of protein and income losses were detailed during the first two years of project implementation. Continued monitoring of the downstream hydrology; piloting, assessment, and adjustment of proposed alternatives; and consultations with villagers proceeded during the construction period. The project called for 50 percent of the downstream programs to have been implemented by commercial operation, and this threshold has been surpassed.

The Nam Theun basin. The river banks along the Nam Theun River are not inhabited between the Nakai Dam and the Theun Hinboun Dam, located 50 kilometers downstream. However, some villages, located nearby on Nam

Theun tributaries, used the river for fishing to varying degrees. The area also has value as a wildlife habitat, as it forms part of the Nakai Nam Theun-Phou Hin Poun Corridor. The NT2 dam would significantly reduce water flows in the area, changing fish habitats, some riparian vegetation, and potentially the use of the area by wildlife. Fisheries and the environment were already under pressure from other causes, including the interruption of fish migration routes by the Theun Hinboun Dam, pollution from mining activities, and inappropriate fishing techniques (blast fishing). Under worst-case scenarios, the impact of the NT2 project on village fish catch was estimated at 10–35 percent in some tributaries and as much as 60 percent in the main course.

Mitigation measures foreseen in the EAMP included outlet structures to reduce water quality impacts and a fish species monitoring program. Provisions were also made for a guaranteed riparian flow regime and in-stream landscaping. Consultations were held with all 40 potentially impacted villages before and during the implementation period. A livelihoods restoration program, similar to that proposed for the Xe Bang Fai, was developed for the affected communities.

Other project lands. Additional project impacts related to the construction of the powerhouse, the dam, and ancillary works, including transmission lines, roads, quarries, and work camps, most of them located in populated areas or areas with degraded habitats. Baseline environmental conditions in these areas, such as air and water quality, were all very good. During the construction period, NT2 could potentially have adverse impacts on water quality and was expected to cause erosion, dust, noise, and vegetation clearing, as well as pressure on biodiversity due to the presence of a large worker population. Minimization of such impacts was addressed through the Head Contractor's Environmental Management and Monitoring Plan. Compensation for land acquisition, resettlement of about 90 households, and impacts on livelihoods in these areas were provided for through resettlement action plans and resettlement frameworks in the SDP.

The Mekong River. The NT2 project will result in changes to the seasonal flows of the Mekong River. These changes are particularly significant between the confluence of the Nam Kading and the Xe Bang Fai rivers, where a reduction in average water levels of 7 centimeters during the wet season and 23–29 centimeters in the dry season is expected. Flows below the confluence of the Xe Bang Fai will also be affected, but they will be attenuated as one moves further downstream. The social, economic, and ecological impacts of these changes are likely to be insignificant.

Potential cumulative impacts of NT2 and other developments (such as other hydropower projects, transport and irrigation projects, and urbanization) likely to occur in the Mekong region were examined through assessment of 5- and 20-year scenarios. NT2 accounts for less than 15 percent of the impacts on Mekong flows in the 5-year scenario and less than 6 percent of the impacts in the 20-year scenario. The assessment concluded that NT2 would have no significant impact on the Mekong sediment balance; an insignificant negative impact on floodplain and Tonle Sap fisheries in Cambodia; and a positive but insignificant impact through reduced flood incidents, improved irrigation, and reduced salt water intrusion in the Mekong delta in Vietnam.

Lessons Learned

Lessons were learned in a variety of areas. A first set of lessons concerns substantive design issues, such as overall problem identification and response, and the definition of approaches, frameworks, and plans to avoid, mitigate, or compensate for negative occurrences while taking advantage of positive opportunities to promote development. Four themes are highlighted here: defining project boundaries, restoring incomes and livelihoods, balancing biodiversity conservation and local development, and addressing downstream risks.

The NT2 experience also sheds light, through a second set of lessons, on related cross-cutting and process issues, such as dealing with uncertainty, addressing institutional challenges, developing suitable consultation and communication strategies, and developing effective monitoring, evaluation, and oversight mechanisms in the context of inevitable tensions and competing private and public sector objectives.

Substantive Design Issues

Defining project boundaries. Defining project boundaries—where the term refers not merely to geographical boundaries but also to project objectives, costs, and institutional responsibilities—turned out to be a vexing issue. The government, the World Bank, and the Bank's development partners saw NT2 in a broader development framework. Beyond ensuring power generation and increased export revenues for Lao PDR, it was hoped that the project's revenues would contribute to poverty reduction, that project benefits would be shared within the project's area of influence, that local capacity would be strengthened in management of environmental and social issues, and that approaches would be generated that might be replicated in future projects. NT2 should not become an "enclave"— the fate of many other large-scale projects in poor economies. For their part, the private developers were understandably concerned with the commercial aspects of the operation, leading to an inherent tension between the government, the World Bank, and the Bank's partners on the one hand, and developers on the other.

The World Bank clearly recognized that the hydropower development project itself could contribute to, but could not be expected to solve, broader development or capacity issues. It therefore sought to address the poverty reduction, regional development, and broader social/environmental objectives through three other complementary instruments.[1] However, in the context of the environmental and social issues of the NT2 project itself, the World Bank insisted that all impacts resulting from the hydropower project needed to be addressed by the developers and mitigation programs paid for within the project's budget. This was the source of frequent discussion. In the absence of agreement, the developers felt that the World Bank was continually expanding boundaries, calling for the design of additional assessments, the establishment of more comprehensive programs, and the expansion of the environmental and social budget—moves it viewed as shifting the goalposts as the project moved ahead.

A few key lessons stand out:

- Proposals for large hydroelectric projects need to be developed in the context of the country's power sector strategy. Strategic social/environmental assessment should be undertaken in advance of site-specific project development so as to minimize the potential impacts and/or maximize the benefits of power sector expansion. The project should be seen as contributing to poverty alleviation and economic development of the region in which it is implemented. These aspects are not normally relevant to a developer's commercial interests; rather, they are matters of public interest and thus government functions.[2]
- Because in large, complex projects, the area in which impacts are felt, and thus the geographical boundaries for environmental and social analytical work, tends to extend beyond the area in which construction activities take place, definition of the project's "area of influence" should be the object of agreement with project proponents early on.

- Early screening and scoping of environmental and social issues through a stakeholder consultation process is advisable and consistent with World Bank policies. Similarly, cumulative impact analysis should be conducted early to better understand the broader geographic context of the proposed project.
- Although early agreement among stakeholders on project boundaries and the approach to be taken to project preparation can prevent protracted disagreements later on, in large, complex projects, it is inevitable that the scope and nature of the issues to be addressed will change as engineering designs and environmental and social assessments become available.

Fortunately, on NT2 all parties agreed early on to include the Nakai–Nam Theun National Protected Area as an offset for biodiversity impacts and thus as an integral part of the project area. There was also early broad agreement on the approach to resettlement and livelihood restoration. These early agreements allowed action on the assessments and plans to be undertaken and clarified the division of responsibilities needed to meet commitments in the case of the plateau and the watershed. In contrast, for the downstream areas, the nature, size, and range of impacts, including the number of people likely to be affected, and the approach for mitigation remained uncertain as late as 2004.

Ensuring income restoration and livelihood enhancement, with special attention to highly vulnerable groups. The NT2 resettlement program was designed to both mitigate and compensate for the effects of the project, by replacing lost assets and improving living conditions for affected communities. The SDP was broad, covering housing, infrastructure, public health, education, community development, income generation, livelihoods restoration and other issues— in line with World Bank policy and international best practice in hydropower development over the past few decades.

A few distinguishing features are worth noting in the NT2 project. First, the people affected by the project were among the poorest and most vulnerable in Lao PDR, making the creation of new patterns of livelihood as well as restoration of lost incomes especially challenging. For this reason, a menu of alternative and complementary livelihood programs (including new forms of agricultural production, fishing, forestry, and harvesting of nontimber forest products) was prepared, piloted and adjusted as the project moved ahead.

Second, because the affected communities were considered Indigenous Peoples, the World Bank's safeguard policies called for preparation of an Ethnic

Minorities Development Plan (EMDP)—which, in the case of NT2, was included within the SDP—and placed specific requirements for culturally appropriate consultation and the design of mitigation/compensation programs. The developers and the government viewed these safeguards as requirements added late in the process. The government was also concerned about the extent to which the affected communities should be entitled to special treatment based on ethnicity. Early consultations were nonetheless effective in identifying cultural practices and preferences that informed the design of relocation sites, village lay-out, and housing solutions.

Third, the developer committed early on to achieve a clear income restoration target. However, uncertainty with respect to key elements of the livelihood package—such as the productivity of reservoir fisheries and the stability of markets for agricultural commodities and timber, as well as the speed of transition to new activities on the part of resettlers—resulted in difficulty in solidifying plans upfront, increasing the reliance on adaptive management and the importance of monitoring and evaluation programs as implementation ensued.

Considerable efforts have been made to restore livelihoods and improve income generation, but the task has been challenging; only time will tell how effective the proposed programs are. Two key lessons emerge for future projects:

- Resettlement of rural communities inevitably entails greater risk and uncertainty than the resettlement of urban communities. Such initiatives thus require early piloting, front-loading of programs, adaptive management, and longer implementation timeframes. NT2 also highlights the critical role of consultation and of monitoring and evaluation, discussed below.
- Proposed income targets (and other binding commitments) need to be carefully assessed for realism and based on solid socioeconomic analysis of local conditions, trends, and comparative experience. Although the World Bank should seek clear commitments, it should play a strong role in avoiding unrealistic promises.

Balancing biodiversity conservation, protection of wildlife habitats, and local development objectives. Early on, the opportunity was identified to protect the Nakai–Nam Theun National Protected Area and two adjoining corridors—a regionally significant biodiversity conservation area nearly 10 times the size of the inundation area—as an offset to the loss of natural habitats arising from the project and as protection of the project watershed, ensuring longevity of the reservoir. Threats to the proposed conservation area were considerable. Moreover, the large numbers of workers and work camp followers expected to migrate to the area to build NT2 posed additional threats.

The offset program consisted of a partnership between NTPC and the government, with long-term financing, innovative institutional arrangements, and a strong capacity-building program. A long-term vision of the protected area was prepared before the start of project implementation, with the objective of ensuring integrity of the area while improving living standards and opportunities for residents of the protected area and surrounding villages. Establishment and strengthening of the Watershed Management and Protection Authority (WMPA) consisted of a long-term technical assistance program in which short-term gaps in diagnostics, planning, and enforcement were addressed through external consultancies. The WMPA hired a highly credible international NGO to assist it. A participatory planning process was promoted that established and fostered adherence to new land- and resource-use patterns and regulations, designed alternative livelihood options to replace activities that were incompatible with conservation, and provided improved access to basic services.

Also early on, the World Bank recognized the need for special purpose wildlife conservation programs. Potential impacts on several important species and significant habitats became a high-visibility issue. However, the assessment and mitigation of project impacts was hampered by lack of adequate baseline data, which forced decisions to be made under difficult circumstances. NTPC conducted detailed and groundbreaking (certainly in the Lao context) fish/freshwater biodiversity surveys in the plateau, watershed, and downstream areas, and developed a detailed wildlife program for the plateau. Contracts were awarded to well-reputed NGOs to establish baselines and design programs for the management of wildlife on the plateau.

To address issues that could undermine the sustainability of the protected area but lay beyond the scope of the NT2 project, the World Bank and the government took parallel action, including a comprehensive program of capacity building and investment in biodiversity conservation in other parts of the country through the Lao Environment and Social Project. In addition, the government reached an agreement with Vietnam on cooperation to control illegal transboundary wildlife trade and logging.

Here again, three early lessons emerge:

- Conservation plans need careful and deep socialization, even among the people assigned to execute and support them, and implementation costs require a realistic assessment. Early agreement on objectives, approaches, division of responsibilities, and notional budgets with stakeholders, particularly private developers, is critical. Without such agreement, innovative and highly desirable conservation plans—such as those achieved in NT2—can cause dissension and delays.
- Wildlife surveys should be conducted early on, because scientifically significant and culturally important habitats and species likely to be affected by the project need early attention. Given the nature of wildlife conservation work, programs should be designed with generous timeframes and adaptive management approaches, often extending well beyond the construction period.
- Government commitment to the long-term vision and effective coordination across sectoral and district authorities to design and implement programs is essential, as is strong but gradual capacity building for the core management authority. In the long run, success in addressing transboundary issues will also be critical.

Addressing downstream risks. Examination of downstream issues has often received limited attention during hydropower planning in the past. As a result, they have been the source of much grievance once projects become operational. In the case of NT2, they presented a vivid example of decision making under uncertainty. Because the level of baseline information was highly variable in quality and reliability and the methodologies for predicting long-term impacts complex, there were many disagreements between the World Bank and the developers. Initially, the developers favored a "wait and see" approach, based on field monitoring and response to problems as they emerged, to be addressed through a modest contingency allocation ($4 million). The World Bank favored a more proactive approach, based on past hydropower development experience and the potential risks, admittedly of varying degrees, to an estimated population of 70,000 people.[3] The World Bank's view was eventually adopted.

Because some types of impacts would predominantly occur only after the start of commercial operations, downstream programs were agreed to at the prefeasibility level before project approval, and detailed during the project construction period. They were designed to be flexible, pilot a menu of solutions, and accommodate changes in stakeholder concerns and experience during project implementation. The base budget included an allocation of $16 million for the downstream program. In addition, a budget of $20 million was allocated for breach of concession agreement obligations and unanticipated impacts, including for the downstream area. A set of other innovative instruments were also foreseen to address project contingencies, as discussed below.

Two key lessons emerge from this experience:

- Downstream impacts are a key aspect of project boundary definition and should be discussed early on. Despite uncertainties, depending on the potential impacts of a project, provision to address such impacts should be made within the project's base budget as well as within the contingency budget.
- Planning needs to be flexible. It should offer a menu of alternatives and allow for piloting, assessment, and adjustment. In rural contexts in which livelihoods need to be reestablished, extended timeframes and corresponding budgets are needed to ensure support to affected people.

Cross-Cutting and Process Issues

Addressing uncertainty through budgets and other legal instruments. There was considerable disagreement between the World Bank and the developer regarding the likelihood and the extent of certain impacts, especially, as noted above, in the downstream areas. This led to a prolonged debate about what mitigation costs should be included as part of the project's base budget. NTPC was reluctant to treat some impacts as foreseeable and thus necessitating the design of mitigation and compensation measures that could be included in appraised plans. It proposed instead what the World Bank considered a modest contingency budget. As discussed, the World Bank favored a proactive approach, with the design of adaptive management programs and inclusion of corresponding budgets upfront. It also argued for a significantly higher contingency budget.

Based on the evidence provided by various studies and advice given by the Environmental and Social Panel of Experts, the International Advisory Group, and the World Bank, the developer ultimately agreed to increase both the base and contingency environmental and social program budgets. As a result, the concession agreement contains clear financial provisions to ensure that environmental and social obligations are met. The base budget considers two types of activities: (a) those limited by scope, such as resettlement and livelihoods restoration, which must be completed regardless of cost, until such time as the objectives of the activity are achieved (or endorsed by the Environmental and Social Panel of Experts) and (b) those limited by cost, where higher degrees of uncertainty exist and the precise scope of work cannot be established upfront. The concession agreement also covers a range of contingencies through the use of letters of credit, performance bonds, and various forms of insurance. A total of $20 million was allocated to address unanticipated impacts and breach of concession agreement obligations; an additional $200 million was foreseen for delay-related contingencies.

Important lessons emerged from this aspect of the project:

- Foreseeable environmental and social project impacts should be addressed through mitigation and compensation programs, and their costs reflected fully in the project's base budget. Financial provisions should recognize that, although some programs can be fully designed upfront, others can only be detailed (and are subject to revision) during implementation.
- A project of the scale and complexity of NT2 can be expected to generate unanticipated environmental and social impacts for which appropriate contingency allocations need to be made.
- Care needs to be taken not to attribute to the project programs that cannot legitimately be linked to project impacts, and are more appropriately dealt with through other instruments and agents (for example, national, regional, or local governments).

Establishing realistic and responsive institutional arrangements. At the start of the project, Lao PDR had limited technical capacity in the management of environmental and social programs. For its part, NTPC was reluctant to accept major direct responsibilities for implementing these programs, which it considered outside its core area of competence. The concession agreement was effectively used to reach common understandings, assigning detailed and differentiated legal responsibilities and obligations to both the government and the developers for implementing environmental and social safeguard measures. Three new government units were established to help the government carry out its responsibilities and obligations—the Resettlement Management Unit (RMU), the Environmental Management Unit (EMU), and the WMPA. The government's RMU and EMU were mirrored by counterpart offices within NTPC. Operational NGOs and international consultants were also involved in various aspects of the environmental and social programs, filling short-term capacity gaps and providing specialized services. At the community level, local institutions (such as village development committees, village forestry associations, and fisher groups) are being strengthened to deal with plateau, watershed, and downstream issues.

Because institutional strengthening takes time, it is too early to judge the success of the arrangements created for the NT2 project. Some lessons have already emerged, however:

- Where the government does not have the necessary capacity, the World Bank has a role to play in building capacity and providing advice. The appropriate locus for the environmental and social safeguard functions needs to be defined; capacity, roles, and responsibilities of agencies realistically assessed and assigned; and strengthening programs designed and implemented. While the project can constitute an important vehicle for capacity building, other instruments may need to be deployed, as was the case in Lao PDR.
- Flexibility to adapt institutional arrangements to evolving circumstances and experience is needed during implementation. Staffing should balance peak demand during implementation and post-implementation requirements. Funding should be provided without straining the availability of grant resources and the government's absorptive capacity.
- Early and clear agreement with developers on their environmental and social responsibilities is critical: private sector developers do not necessarily share the government's objectives, and they often consider implementation of environmental and social programs outside their area of competence, despite evolving best practice. However, responsibility for addressing the project's impacts, achieving plan and program objectives, ensuring compliance with the project's policies and guidelines, and assuming the costs thereof must rest in full with the developer, regardless of arrangements it may choose to establish for delivery of mitigation and compensation programs (for instance, through third parties).

Engaging in participatory consultation and transparent communications throughout the project cycle. These activities are essential to the effective management of environmental and social programs in a complex project such as NT2. However, they pose special challenges in a context such as Lao PDR. At the start of the project in the 1990s (see chapter 4), community representatives and NGOs complained that communications were one-way flows of information, and were often misunderstood by local communities. Affected people, they claimed, were not given development alternatives but simply informed of their resettlement entitlements, with little opportunity to express concerns.

Beginning in 1997, training in consultation skills, the assumption of a more prominent role by the government, and the public release of key studies improved consultation processes. Over time, given delays in project preparation, there were complaints of "consultation overload" at the local level.

Consultation efforts undertaken in 2004–05 addressed earlier criticisms, striving for more balanced, meaningful exchanges of information. Specialists were mobilized to improve the design of the process, develop appropriate materials to support discussions of issues and options, train facilitators, and carry out consultations in all plateau villages and a representative number of watershed and downstream communities. Despite these efforts, criticism of and debate over the adequacy of consultation remain.

NT2 attracted an enormous amount of international attention, generating comments and questions from numerous sources and countries. The World Bank and its partners assisted the government and developers in establishing a transparent communication strategy, which included dedicated Web sites, periodic updates on frequently asked questions, and national and international consultations the year before NT2 was presented to the World Bank's Board. During implementation, a similarly transparent approach has been pursued. National and international NGOs have access to the project site, and annual stakeholder workshops are held. NT2 ultimately represents a ground-breaking initiative with respect to consultation and communications in the Lao PDR.

The main lessons that emerge are as follows:

- Consultation and communication strategies need to be defined early and pursued throughout the project cycle. For safeguards, the first challenge that needs to be addressed is the scoping process—determining how to obtain stakeholder views on the project's area of influence, critical topics for study, and appropriate roles for national and international civil society organizations and NGOs. Consultations with affected people should proceed during the design and implementation phases, to ensure that arrangements are adequate and responsive to local needs as they become increasingly detailed and operationalized.
- The roles of the government and the developer in consultations with affected peoples and external stakeholders with diffuse interests should be clearly defined. It is essential that the project be "owned," and thus consultations be led, by project proponents and not their consultants.
- Consultation needs to be meaningful. Specialized input may be necessary to design methodologies sensitive to social, linguistic, and ethnic differ-

ences. External monitoring can play an important role in assessing the credibility and effectiveness of the consultation process in a context of skepticism of the process.

Engaging in internal and external project monitoring. Hydropower projects are highly complex and involve considerable risk, especially when implemented in a political and economic context such as Lao PDR. Because baseline information and key assessments are often lacking and take time to establish, it is not possible to identify all programs upfront. Because mitigation and compensation measures are meant to address communities with differing degrees of coping and adaptation capacities, adaptive management becomes a strategic necessity. Flexibility to adapt to new information is essential.

In this context, both internal and external monitoring and evaluation and the advice of respected independent outside experts can be invaluable. International stakeholders demand open, transparent, independent mechanisms to monitor project performance and report on the results of large-scale infrastructure projects that are perceived as high risk, but not all parties agree on what this entails. For NT2, several layers of external monitoring were put in place. These included (a) the Environmental and Social Panel of Experts, the Dam Safety Review Panel, and the Government Engineer, to provide expert advice to the government overall; (b) independent monitoring agencies, to oversee and advise on the activities of the government units; and (c) the Lenders' Technical Advisor and the International Advisory Group, to advise financiers on implementation progress.

Four key lessons emerge from this aspect of the NT2 experience:

- Monitoring and evaluation commitments need to be long-term. In the case of NT2, the Environmental and Social Panel of Experts will be active for the full concession period; the Lenders' Technical Advisor will be in place for 17 years.
- Entirely independent monitoring—that is, monitoring that does not rely on any of the project implementing parties for funding—cannot be the basis for regular monitoring and evaluation.
- Although the layers of external monitoring put in place for NT2 proved useful in providing critical advice to developers and gaining acceptance for programs by other partners, the developer had legitimate concerns that too many monitoring bodies, with overlapping responsibilities, had been established.

- Structuring monitoring roles by function (that is, regular data collection, data verification, oversight, and advisory) rather than by lines of reporting (for example, to the developer, the government, the international financial institutions) may reduce duplication of efforts and help ensure that internal and external monitoring are complementary rather than parallel activities.

Project Economic Analysis

Once an arcane niche of applied benefit-cost analysis of interest only to its practitioners and the boards of financing institutions, project economics has taken center stage in the preparation of large infrastructure projects over the past decade. NT2 epitomized the key economic issues that many major projects face.

The main issues that arose in NT2 included the following:

- Was the project needed by the proposed commissioning date or indeed at any other time far into the future? At the time the project was conceived, the Electricity Generating Authority of Thailand (EGAT), the main purchaser of power from NT2, had a large surplus of electrical capacity. Project critics believed that demand forecasts in Thailand were exaggerated and that there was ample scope for reducing electricity use by more effective conservation and demand management. The construction of new power plants, they argued, could be put off until far into the future.
- Was the project consistent with the least-cost strategy for expanding Thailand's power supply? EGAT was operating a very large and successful power production program using combined-cycle gas turbines (CCGT) with attractively priced natural gas from domestic, shared, and imported resources. The NT2 power contract itself helped fuel this debate, because the power was priced to be competitive with the then-perceived future costs of EGAT's natural gas option. Hence, the two options looked similar—on the surface.
- Would there be enough value-added from NT2's power production to, at a minimum, compensate the project's environmental and social impacts in Lao PDR?
- How likely was the project to remain economically viable over time? The sustainability of long-term contracts partly depends on the contracting parties continuing to perceive that the project is to their mutual advantage. A factor

that contributes to this perception is the project's ongoing economic advantage. If a perception were to develop that needs could be satisfied in better ways, this would weaken the contractual underpinnings of the project.

Forecasting Demand for Electricity

One of the very first controversial issues surrounding the project was whether EGAT really needed the capacity—that is, whether or not it had paid adequate attention to demand risks, energy conservation, and the rehabilitation of its existing capacity. Although the project is large, the Thai power system is very much larger, and it was growing (by 6.5 percent per year over the 1993–2003 period). The World Bank used the official forecast (August 2002) of the Thailand Load Forecast Subcommittee as the base case demand forecast, after examining its construction and its coherence with performance in the recent past and with the country's broader economic performance.

The circumstance of concern in 2003 was that by the World Bank's calculations, Thailand had a capacity surplus of about 3,500 MW over the reserve it needed for power system reliability. The surplus was caused by the decline in growth of demand caused by the Asian financial crisis of 1997. Because the system was large (peak load of 19,325 MW in 2004) and demand growth had resumed by the end of the 1990s, however, moderate rates of growth applied to a large base would quickly erode the surplus: the World Bank projected that the surplus would be gone by 2006 and that the system would need additional capacity to meet its energy requirements and reliability criteria. The 920 MW net of power for Thailand produced by NT2 would be fully utilized within less than one year from the projected commissioning date, and it would provide only about 6 percent of Thailand's energy demand growth over 2009–16. The World Bank was also able to satisfy itself that EGAT had a sound technical and economic process for selecting its plant retirements and rehabilitation projects and that taking its overall investment program into account, the additional capacity represented by NT2 was well timed for the planned commissioning date.

As for demand management and energy-efficiency programming, the load forecast included 928 MW of savings. The World Bank commissioned a study on electricity conservation and demand management to verify the reasonableness of this estimate. This study indicated a reliable savings potential of 2,207 MW at peak, or 1,279 MW more than already included in the Thai forecast of 928 MW savings. The effectiveness of demand management and energy-efficiency programming depends on decisions made by millions of consumers; for good reason, power planners treat this potential conservatively to guard against the risk of insufficient supply. Even if demand management succeeded in reducing demand by an additional 1,279 MW, however, demand growth over the 2003–09 period would decline only marginally, from the base case 6.2 percent per year to 6.0 percent per year, delaying the optimal commissioning date of NT2 by less than one year. The World Bank's risk analysis also tested the project's viability at 3.4 percent annual demand growth, as discussed next, hence the potential for much enhanced demand management and conservation was covered in the risk-analysis scenarios.

Considering Alternate Sources of Supply

The next major controversy concerned supply alternatives. Why build a project like NT2, with all of its in situ impacts and long-distance transmission, when Thailand had a large, successful, and economic program of electricity production from CCGT plants based on inexpensive supplies of natural gas? Answering this question represented an important aspect of the economic analysis, because there was a wide range of views inside and outside the World Bank about natural gas supply, price development, and economic valuation. In addition, in the natural gas industry, there is much natural and manmade opacity about the longer-term outlook for certain key parameters that affect valuation. The controversies were intellectually interesting, but the World Bank needed to settle on a practical and credible approach to natural gas valuation.

Normally, in applying natural resource economics to valuing an exhaustible asset, one charges the resource with a depletion premium (or "user cost"), provided one has adequate confidence about the timing and extent of increasing scarcity value and the timing and value of a backstop (substitute) on the resource's economic exhaustion. The lower the estimated scarcity value, the farther ahead in time it may occur; the lower the expected cost, the farther away the reliance on a backstop; and the lower the certainty about these conditions, the less compelling the case is for calculating and assigning user costs. Information collected in Thailand and the World Bank's oil price outlooks at the time suggested that the World Bank should not build user costs into the economic valuation of the resource, especially as it was seeking to avoid overstating the cost of viable alternatives to NT2.

Using border prices[4] is a routine way of estimating the economic value of internationally tradable commodities, but natural gas often entails substantial transportation costs, and—depending on the usage—conversion costs, both of which are subtracted from end-use value to obtain the netback value to the resource itself. Combined with contracting factors governing certain usage (having to do with contract quantities, minimum takes, pipeline reservation fees, floors and ceilings on price variability, as well as other provisions), this often mitigates a lock-step flow-through of world oil prices to natural gas prices. Thai resource managers had concluded that using the country's own gas deposits for domestic electricity production would yield the highest netback to the resource. They also informed the World Bank that their domestic reserves would be produced along with an import component from neighboring countries, ensuring long-term supply to the domestic market from both sources on reasonable terms.

Using this information, the World Bank developed the valuation basis from a combination of World Bank oil price forecasts, contracting practices in the region that define mutually agreed valuation between buyers and sellers of gas, and other proprietary information that natural gas producers and users in Thailand provided to the World Bank, with understandings on confidentiality. The economic gas values were below commercial prices, for several reasons:

- As economic resource costs, they exclude transfers (income taxes and royalties) on the Thai portion of the gas supply.
- Economic pipeline tolls are well below commercial tolls, because the economic marginal cost of gas pipeline transportation is limited to recurrent operating cost, the capital charge component for both existing infrastructure and facilities then under construction being sunk costs.
- Given the proven/probable reserves estimate and the minimum ratio between the stock of proved and probable reserves relative to the annual production flow adopted, extensive reliance on incremental volumes of imported gas should not begin until after the end of the system expansion period required for the least-cost analysis (2004–14). Thereafter, the extent and incremental costs of imported gas or newly discovered and developed domestic gas are difficult to ascertain with confidence. The economic natural gas values the World Bank calculated may well understate eventual long-term economic values. If they do, they more severely test the comparative economic merit of the NT2 project, in the sense that the less expensive the natural gas power generation option appears to be, the less expensive the NT2 project must be in order to be positioned within a

least-cost power generation strategy. The low-case and high-case spreads
from the base case were developed by taking the values of oil at one standard deviation above and below the World Bank's base case oil price forecast current at the time and working these changes through the generic
contractual gas-pricing formula characterizing much of the contracting
between EGAT and the gas producers. The World Bank also included the
assumed variance of the import share to calculate the range. This resulted
in a long-term economic supply price of natural gas to the power sector of
about $2.00–$2.57/mmbtu.

Measuring the Economic Costs of Environmental and Social Impacts

Given the high level of concern about environmental and social costs both
inside and outside the World Bank, the developer group knew from the start
that this set of issues could be a deal-breaker. To prevent potential problems,
it went to great lengths to address it. In addition, as a condition of financing,
the World Bank required that its environmental and social guidelines be met.[5]

The World Bank's economics team reviewed all the data it could retrieve
from studies on environmental and social costs and benefits. It estimated
the present value of environmental and social costs at about $54 million
over the contractual life of the project. The developers had estimated about
$64 million present value for these costs. The World Bank, therefore, used
the developer's estimate.

This exercise also identified about $40 million present value of prospective
incremental environmental and social benefits that most likely would be un-
realized without the project. Consistent with the World Bank's desire not to
overstate the project's benefits, it did not credit the project with these potential benefits. It is important to note that the project may facilitate them,
however. If one puts the environmental and social costs and benefits in
perspective, the economic cost of the NT2 project in the base case was about
$1 billion; including the environmental and social costs, it was projected to
create $266 million net present value savings of power supply costs over the
next best alternative without the project.

Assessing Long-Run Sustainability

The base case net present value cost advantage of NT2 looked very good.
Before the project was approved, however, the risks to the project's long-term

economic value needed to be carefully examined. To do so, the World Bank developed a cost-risk analytic framework. The purpose of this analysis was to test whether a decision to start constructing NT2 in 2005 for an expected commercial operations date of end-2009 (the "NT2 Option") versus not implementing it would be robust to a range of alternative outcomes for the key factors that could change and affect the net present value of the NT2 option. The context was that once the Power Purchase Agreement (PPA) was signed, a series of commitments with onerous penalties for nonfulfill-ment would make it very difficult to alter the commercial operations date. The same assumption applied to the other plant EGAT had defined as firmly committed. In contrast, other planned additions were insufficiently com-mitted and far enough in the future that there was time to recognize both the need for altering their commercial operations date and the feasibility of doing so.

Hydrologic risk is a prominent feature of many hydroelectric projects. In the case of NT2, it was assessed not to be, for two reasons. First, based on in-tensive, long-term hydrological studies, the project was dimensioned to sub-stantially break the linkage between variable water flows and deliveries of en-ergy and payments. Second, the PPA had a complex mechanism for ensuring that contracted primary energy amounts would be delivered and payments sustained on a rolling multiyear basis.

The three factors the World Bank determined could have the greatest im-pact on the net present value of the NT2 option were the project costs, the demand forecast, and the value of natural gas. The cost-risk analysis recog-nized that the values of these factors were uncorrelated and that any combi-nation of higher and lower values between them could occur. The objective was to determine whether on balance the NT2 option had a positive net pres-ent value (at a 10 percent discount rate) relative to the alternative decision to not build the project, thus taking into account all the tested risk values for these factors and the probabilities of occurrence of all their combinations.

The probabilities of occurrence of any one combination of these factors de-pend on the number of possible combinations of the factors and the individ-ual probabilities of occurrence assigned to the high, base, and low values for each factor. The probabilities of occurrence and the variance of parameter values at those probabilities of occurrence were selected by using two consid-erations: (a) experience of how the values of key factors had varied from ex-pected values in other relevant project situations and (b) the need to choose probabilities of occurrence that maintained the base case as the most probable option, even if only by a small margin relative to any other tested conditions. The remainder of the process consisted of identifying the cases of particular interest to the NT2 evaluation. This selection was made by using (a) estimates of the net present value of the base case with and without NT2, (b) understanding of the extent to which adverse values for NT2 put the economic worth of the project at risk, and (c) definition of the minimum conditions for the project as part of the least-cost system expansion program relative to the next best alternative for meeting the load without the project.

The present value of each tested pair of cases (that is, with and without NT2) was calculated using EGAT's system expansion planning model. The results indicated a base case present value saving of $266 million for the NT2 option, a minimum 86 percent probability of achieving a lower net present value cost than its natural gas–based alternative, and only an 11 percent probability of not achieving it.

Satisfied that the project could form part of a least-cost power system expansion strategy with good prospects for sustainability, the World Bank turned to examining its value added. The fact that a project is the least-cost way of producing electricity does not necessarily mean that its value to the end users of electricity exceeds its cost. That remained to be determined, using an expected internal rate of return (EIRR) approach.

Economic Rate of Return

The EIRR analytical framework was designed to find the EIRR of a series of annual economic costs and benefits. Benefits consist of the value of project energy to end users. Costs include constructing and operating the project, delivering the project's energy to end users through transmission and distribution systems, and managing environmental and social impacts.

The estimated project (base case) EIRR was 16.3 percent. This EIRR applies to the economic net benefit flow over a 30-year period from start of construction to the end of the PPA. The environmental and social costs incurred during the investment period (2005–09) were included as investment costs; those incurred during the project operational period (2010–34) were included as operating costs. A major hydro project should have a longer benefit stream. Although heavily discounted, its inclusion would increase the EIRR moderately. The period beyond the 30th year was not included, however, because of the uncertainty about off-take arrangements beyond the duration of the PPA.

The World Bank also tested the sensitivity of the EIRR to a range of possible circumstances that could impair the project's economic value added. These included project delay, cost overruns, low demand (the Thai system low load growth rate assumed in the cost-risk analysis), hydrological distress in 2010 and 2011 equivalent to the worst two hydrological years on record (notwithstanding developer assurance of near certainty that the reservoir will be filled before commissioning), and various combinations of these adverse circumstances. The World Bank found that the most sensitive disruption factor was demand—not an unusual finding for this kind of project. Even a worst-case scenario, combining low demand growth with a 30 percent cost overrun, did not bring the EIRR below 10 percent, however. On this basis, the World Bank was satisfied that the project EIRR was robust.

Lessons Learned

Economic due diligence was designed and undertaken using meticulously crafted assumptions and projections to robustly test a range of multi-factor scenarios that could affect the economic attractiveness and viability of NT2. Several lessons emerge, especially on how to design and undertake such analyses so that the resulting information is understandable and useful to a variety of stakeholders.

Conduct far-reaching economic analysis. A set of intensive analytical processes and dialogues within and beyond the World Bank endured for more than two years, as new issues emerged that required revisiting various assumptions. The economic analysis—which was unusually far-reaching because of the project's controversial history—drew on numerous types of information that developed in parallel as part of a much broader spectrum of project preparation activities.

Engage a broad range of expertise. The generous assistance of many groups facilitated the economic analysis. Because about 95 percent of the project's power and energy was contracted to EGAT, the Thai power market was the most critical locus of power sector analysis for all but the environmental and social factors. The fact that Thailand's power sector institutions are strong, competent, and efficient made it practical and sensible to engage their expertise on much of the power market analyses needed for this appraisal.

In Lao PDR, Electricité du Laos, the government, NTPC, and Lahmeyer International GmbH (the engineering company) provided data on the hydrological characteristics of the project, its development risks, generation expansion options for Lao PDR, the future development and integration of the retail power market, and the PPA. NTPC provided useful insight and data on project costs, including environmental and social costs, hydrologic risks, and the structure and assumptions for the costs and revenues in the project financial model.

The World Bank engaged a strong team that drew heavily on local or near-local resources and expertise. Besides World Bank staff, the team included both a consultant engineer and an economic consultant on electric power systems, both with deep and lengthy experience of the Thai and Lao power systems; a consultant on environmental economics with considerable experience in the East Asia region; other consultants who provided advice on specific engineering matters for both the project and CCGT technology and some risk-sharing provisions of the PPA; and a team leader. In addition to overall coordination of project economic analysis, the team leader focused much of his effort on the outlook for natural gas supply in Thailand, where gas-fired generators were the main alternative to hydro. In collaboration with team members, including several World Bank staff specialists, he developed the integrating frameworks for conducting the least-cost, EIRR, and risk analyses.

Hold consultations on project economics. The analytic process also involved meetings with NGOs and some experienced private sector experts about project economics at several stages, including in workshops in Vientiane, Bangkok, Tokyo, Paris, and Washington. NGOs' concerns about project economics focused mainly on the issues identified above. The World Bank studied their submissions and discussed them with staff. Most of the debate with NGOs focused on the assumptions underlying the various strands of analytic work. The main difference between their perspectives and those of the World Bank was that their arguments rested heavily on their often unfavorable assumptions about the project, whereas the project team focused on the robustness of the project to a range of both favorable and unfavorable future events possibly affecting the project's prospective viability. The World Bank's definition of assumption ranges drew from its own research, from the accumulated experience of its staff, from the experience of relevant private sector operators, and from advice provided by NGOs.

Because the World Bank conducted probabilistic analyses using a wide range of values for the key assumptions, there were overlaps between some of the NGO basic positions and the World Bank's ranges. Although a long series of consultations and exchanges with the NGOs did not lead to agreement on all points, it did leave both sides with an understanding of the other side's perspective.

Recognize the critical importance of assumptions. Four years after the development of the major assumptions underlying this work, the world evolved in ways that no one ever dreamed of, let alone considered and dismissed as too improbable to analyze. The World Bank examined a range of assumptions that lay within reasonable expectations of potential occurrence at the time, not to deal with sea changes of the kind witnessed beginning in 2008. The massive increases in commodity, fossil fuel, and equipment prices that occurred especially in 2007/2008; the crammed order books of the world's major infrastructure providers; and the very difficult project bidding conditions this situation entails were impossible to predict in 2004. The environment of commodity inflation that occurred well into 2008 and the extent of the subsequent international financial and economic downturns all exceeded expectations thought plausible at the time the World Bank appraised NT2 (2004/2005).

Retrospective analyses conducted as part of the World Bank's project completion process often address two related questions. First, given recent experience, do conventional views about reasonable boundaries of risk analysis remain adequate for having confidence in a range of future outcomes? Second, how useful is it to depend on forecasts, however elaborate and whatever the assumption ranges, for project evaluation? In the case of NT2, the cost protection built in to the contracting structure and the effect of recent events on world hydrocarbon markets played in the project's favor; a prolonged recession does not.

The Financial Package for NT2

The NT2 project financing presented the challenge of raising a considerable amount of commercial debt in support of a large, complex infrastructure project in a small, poor country with limited creditworthiness. This was not a unique challenge; however, it was met in an innovative way.

Designing Suitable Financial Instruments

Through a mix of multilateral guarantee instruments (debt guarantees provided by the International Development Association [IDA], the World Bank Group's Multilateral Investment Guarantee Agency [MIGA], and the Asian Development Bank [ADB]) and modest direct lending, the international financial institutions participating in the NT2 financing were able to leverage moderate amounts of public resources to mobilize more than $1.15 billion in limited-recourse private funding. NT2 was the first IDA guarantee in support of hydropower development. It was also the first project to use a mix of IDA, MIGA, and ADB guarantees. The mix of guarantees helped provide the necessary comfort to leverage investment in NT2, facilitating attainment of the needed level of borrowing. All large and complex infrastructure projects, particularly in poor countries with limited creditworthiness, could benefit from the use of such multilateral guarantee mechanisms.

The World Bank's intervention raised the creditworthiness of Lao PDR and made it possible for international lenders and private developers to seriously consider taking Lao risk for future private sector projects without multilateral guarantees. (Preliminary proposals have already been made to EGAT for a number of cross-border energy projects for supply of power to Thailand without the involvement of multilateral institutions.) A successful financial package like that created for NT2 also helps facilitate refinancing after construction of other projects in the country, as was successfully done for the Theun Hinboun hydropower project.

The large size of the financing package for NT2 was possible because of a confluence of favorable factors that may not always be present in other country situations. These factors included the involvement of a very reputable international company (Electricité de France [EdF]), the favorable economics of NT2, the existing regional understandings on water and power, and a creditworthy off-taker (EGAT).

Mobilizing a Broad Range of Financiers

With support from the World Bank and the government, NTPC involved a variety of multilateral and bilateral financial institutions. Nine multilaterals, bilaterals, and export credit agencies provided $130 million of direct loans and $108 million to fund the government's equity contribution. In addition,

$340 million of international lending was covered by guarantees provided by them. The equity shares in NT2 were as follows: Electricité de France International (EdFI), 35 percent; the Italian Thai Development Public Company (ITD), 15 percent; the Electricity Generating Public Company of Thailand (EGCO), 25 percent; and the Lao PDR government, 25 percent. By agreement among the various partners involved, an innovative package was put together to fund the required government equity, with grants from IDA, the Agence Française du Développement (AFD), and loans from the European Investment Bank (EIB) and ADB.

The World Bank and other international financial institutions provided high-quality technical work that other partners could build on for much of the due diligence work, particularly in the areas of environmental and social safeguards, revenue management, and monitoring and evaluation. ADB and AFD joined the project only in 2003; MIGA joined in 2004. These institutions built on the due diligence work that the World Bank and other commercial financiers had undertaken, as did other official agencies, including EIB, the Nordic Investment Bank, the Guarantee Institute for Export Credits (GIEK), COFACE, Proparco, Exportkreditnamnden (EKN), and the Thai Exim Bank. Early in the process, clear agreements were reached with the other partners to define areas of work responsibility, with each taking primary responsibility for different areas. The World Bank worked in close partnership with ADB and AFD, conducting joint missions on key issues, drafting joint aide-mémoires, writing joint letters to the government and NTPC, and supporting international workshops.

Coordinating Due Diligence

Significant efforts were made to harmonize the safeguard requirements of various institutions. A schedule was added to the Common Terms Agreement between the commercial lenders and NTPC that covenanted NTPC to apply this single common set of principles. The project financing package was conditioned on common environmental and social principles subscribed to by all lenders, so that a default by NTPC on environmental and social matters leads to a default on all the commercial, bilateral, and multilateral components of the financing package.

The export credit agencies also worked well together. COFACE negotiated an "export credit policy" with the developers; GIEK and EKN backstopped

COFACE under separate "guarantee" agreements. As a result, the developers did not have to negotiate separate agreements with each of the export credit agencies.

Addressing Country Risks

The World Bank Group's and ADB's role in providing guarantees was critical in raising substantial private funding. About $42 million in IDA political risk guarantees, $42 million in ADB guarantees, and MIGA guarantees for debt ($85.6 million, covering $42 million of principal) and equity ($5 million) attracted about $1.15 billion of private investment and lending in NT2—an impressive level of leverage. In addition, a $500 million equivalent Thai baht financing was arranged to match the 50/50 dollar/baht currency split of the revenue stream.

The IDA guarantee provides cover only for Lao political risk; it does not cover Thai political risk. The Thai political risk of the off-take arrangements is held by the private parties, including the Thai commercial banks, which are also uncovered for Lao political risks. The Thai political risk for private international dollar lenders is backed only by MIGA and ADB guarantees and by cover from export credit agencies. NTPC was charged an annual fee of 2 percent for the IBRD enclave guarantee operation, in addition to a processing fee of $5 million to recover the higher than usual project preparation costs.

At the request of NTPC, the international commercial banks, which provided $326 million for NT2, participated as a "club deal" rather than through a lead arranger. Because of their earlier relations with some of the commercial banks, the government and NTPC wanted to deal directly with them rather than through a lead arranger. As is normal in such large projects, the commercial banks as a group appointed their own engineering, legal, and insurance experts and agreed on an allocation of major tasks. As a result, despite the existence of a large number of banks, discussions with the banks were relatively smooth.

It is interesting to contrast the credit-enhancement mechanisms used in NT2 and the Chad-Cameroon pipeline project, which did not have an IDA guarantee but used the presence of the International Finance Corporation with an A and a B loan and the participation of the World Bank as a lender to provide comfort to commercial lenders. The Chad-Cameroon project could be financed without multilateral guarantees because oil projects are more marketable than hydropower projects and the potential for higher oil prices provides more of an upside potential for the developers, thereby providing a cushion for project lenders. Moreover, the oil companies in the Chad-Cameroon project provided a significantly larger share of equity in the financing package than in NT2, which reduced the risk from the commercial lenders' point of view.

Perceptions of Financial Partners

As in all infrastructure transactions, the partners in NTPC had different interests and points of view. As the major equity partner and head contractor, EdF had a dominant position and thus the most to gain or lose in all aspects of the project. In addition to having a smaller equity interest, ITD was a subcontractor under the head contract. It was content to play a supporting role and to let EdF take the lead on most issues. EGCO's interest was solely as an equity partner; it did not benefit from any contractual awards. It was thus most sensitive to cost considerations, including the construction and consulting costs incurred by its other partners. Both EGCO and ITD were in a privileged position to handle any issues that arose in Thailand. For its part, the government of Lao PDR, in addition to its equity share, was interested in the macro and micro impacts of the project and was under pressure to fulfill a number of World Bank conditions related to revenue and financial management and other macro framework issues. It was also sensitive to potential conflicts between the demands of a private sector–led project and its centrally managed system.

Involvement of World Bank staff. NT2 could not have been financed without the involvement of the World Bank—as all parties involved in the project agree. It was impossible to obtain $1.4 billion from multilateral and bilateral sources for Lao PDR; the developers realized that risk mitigation through political risk guarantees from multilateral agencies would be essential to attract private commercial funds. The World Bank Group's and ADB's role in providing guarantees was critical and appreciated by the developers. They also appreciated that the World Bank, through the successful financial closure of NT2, raised the creditworthiness of Lao PDR and made it possible for international lenders and private developers to seriously consider taking Lao risk for future private sector projects without guarantees from the World Bank (and in some cases without risk mitigation by other institutions, such as ADB, MIGA, or export credit agencies).

Value of World Bank environmental and social safeguards. Most partners agreed with the overall environmental and social standards applied by the World Bank, which was viewed as uniquely qualified to promote such standards. Moreover, the standards were ultimately found to be appropriate for NT2 in most respects. In fact, with minor variations, most partners would like to find a way to apply these standards to future projects—even in cases in which the World Bank is not directly involved. At the same time, some expressed a view that the process could have been more efficient.

Partnership with ADB and AFD. Both the World Bank and ADB view their joint work as one of the best collaborations they have engaged in. There were important complementarities in the relationship. ADB, which is Lao PDR's second-largest donor and which maintained a consistent presence in infrastructure in the country during the difficult years, enjoyed greater trust by the government and better understood the sociopolitical situation. For its part, the World Bank had already done much of the technical and due diligence work before ADB joined. ADB was comfortable following the World Bank's lead, with clear agreement on the split of work between the two institutions. It was thus relatively easy to reach agreements on work-sharing by the World Bank and ADB. The partnership with AFD was also a constructive one, although AFD expressed some concerns about the efficiency of World Bank processes.

Relationship with the government and NTPC. Throughout most of the earlier project preparation period, the government was concerned about compromising its principles and worried about the encroachment on its sovereignty. NTPC also found the World Bank's project management too loose, with multiple missions and expert visits not fully coordinated with one another.

The quality of interactions changed in 2003, when the government's level of trust in the World Bank and its approach to NT2 increased markedly. A few senior officials played a key role in this transformation. The persistence and patience of the World Bank staff and the support of key World Bank managers were also critical. With greater and more direct participation by sector management, NTPC felt that the World Bank's interactions with it were clearer and reflected tighter teamwork and more orderly project management.

In 2003, the World Bank prepared and gained agreement from the government on a matrix of actions, which was very useful in providing clarity and specificity of expectations and in tracking progress by participants. However, the World Bank was perceived as adding demands and continually revising the matrix in subsequent months. The government and NTPC were more comfortable with each other after the concession agreement was signed and provided greater clarity in their roles. EdF officials said that they would have preferred earlier World Bank involvement in the definition of the concession agreement.

NTPC also complained about the 2 percent guarantee fee charged by IDA, which was more than twice what IDA usually charges and which raised its cost of international borrowing. NTPC was also unhappy about having to reimburse the World Bank $5 million for the high preparation cost, and it believes the fee was imposed very late in the project preparation process. For its part, the World Bank believed that it had communicated with NTPC that fees would be charged for processing and that the fees were likely to be significant; in its view, it could not officially and publicly have demanded a particular fee earlier in the process, because doing so would have implied its formal commitment to NT2. The fees were used to finance intensive supervision of the project by the World Bank. During implementation, this served the interests of NTPC well.

EdF felt that the delineation between project, regional, and national boundaries was not always clear in the World Bank's conditions and that at any rate many World Bank staff did not respect such delineation. They considered the decision framework articulated by the country director helpful in this regard.

The World Bank's handling of the environmental and social safeguards exasperated NTPC. The most frequent complaint related to World Bank processes and the length of time taken for decision making. NTPC was frustrated by the lack of predictability about where the World Bank stood on particular aspects of the environmental and social standards, shifting goal posts, and uncertainty about when the World Bank would finally articulate its position and who was really in charge of resolving issues as they arose. The frustration was heightened by the sheer number of missions and experts on environmental and social issues visiting at different times, generating a continuous flow of documents. None of the partners felt that it had the staff or skills to keep up with the mission and information overload.

NT2 is a project with unusually good economics (and thus an ability to absorb high environmental and social mitigation costs that other projects may be unable to bear). Nevertheless, its environmental and social budget is in line with international experience of the last 15–20 years, with a total environmental and social budget of about 10 percent of total project costs, of which about 85–90 percent is allocated to resettlement.

Ultimately, it was not the total financial cost or the standards of the environmental and social requirements that troubled the developers and other partners. NTPC felt that it would have preferred knowing the standards expected up front. In hindsight, it would have preferred to assume only the financial responsibility for the costs of environmental and social mitigation measures, not the responsibility for their implementation and management, which posed a heavy burden. NTPC was created to be a hydropower company, with limited expertise on environmental and social measures. Under NT2, it was required to beef up its capacity to handle such matters. It initially had an open-ended financial commitment to fund certain mitigation programs; this commitment was ultimately capped for each of the mitigation areas, following agreement between the government and the World Bank.

World Bank environmental and social managers and staff have different perceptions from those of the developers. The World Bank has policies, principles, and recommended approaches and processes, which should take into account the specific context in which they are applied. These policies need to be interpreted by experienced professionals. According to World Bank staff, guidance was repeatedly provided in successive missions, aide-mémoires, and reviews of documentation; its view was that the developers were not willing to fully address the issues until very late in the game, leading to delays in project preparation and high costs to all concerned. Perhaps in their relative inexperience of environmental and social issues, the developers thought that the World Bank's concerns could be satisfied with a few easy fixes, such as the high standard of housing and the income target they proposed to adopt.

Despite significant attempts at coordination and harmonization, developers and financial institutions sometimes complained about differences in the standards and procedures of the World Bank, ADB, and export credit agencies, particularly regarding environmental and social issues. The public and private partners reported no problems accessing World Bank information and transaction documents as needed; they did complain about the lack of efficiency of World Bank processes relating to timeliness of information flows and World Bank decision making. Once the World Bank put coordination arrangements in place, information flowed, albeit sometimes belatedly.

In the perception of NTPC, the World Bank did not fully commit to its participation in the project until just before Board approval, forcing NTPC to spend significant up-front resources without a clear understanding regarding World Bank involvement. Without clear and formal institutional signals of the World Bank's ultimate involvement, the burden of providing comfort to the developers and other financiers was put on the World Bank staff and managers involved. They informally indicated the high likelihood of World Bank involvement if the decision framework principles were adequately met. Informal channels helped only up to a point, however. Both public and private partners needed senior World Bank management to articulate its position.

The World Bank's point of view was that the final commitment on its involvement in a project can be provided only at the time of Board approval. Moreover, World Bank management perceived some ambivalence regarding NT2 among major shareholders of the World Bank. Coupled with the intense international scrutiny of large hydropower projects, this made senior management extremely reluctant to publicly commit the institution's involvement in NT2 until its due diligence had been completed and all the conditions of the decision framework had been fully met.

The frustration of the developers and others seemed to stem in part from their perception that the World Bank did not fully appreciate the constraints under which private sector projects are prepared. The private sector needs more predictable budget and cost estimates upfront; developers had serious problems with the open-ended commitments the World Bank seemed to impose on them. They also reported that World Bank missions did not have adequate understanding of the monitoring and evaluations requirements of private sector projects.

The government and the developers believed that the balance in NT2 went too far toward excessive and expensive policy leverage. The transaction costs of dealing with the World Bank were too high and the burden placed on key officials onerous.

The risk-management proposal discussed below may provide a possible solution to meet the needs of both the World Bank and the private sector in future projects.

Lessons Learned

The World Bank's involvement in NT2 yields both positive lessons of experience and suggestions for how the World Bank could improve its performance in other large-scale infrastructure projects in poor countries. Positive lessons include the following:

- It can be worthwhile to "stay the course" despite an adverse international environment and significant changes over time. Ultimate engagement in the project avoided the reputational damage to the World Bank (and repercussions to a number of its shareholders, with country ties to different aspects of the project) that would have been associated with pulling out after having conducted significant work.
- Projects should use multilateral guarantee mechanisms to leverage resources in large and complex projects, particularly in countries with limited creditworthiness. Even in a poor country with limited financial and human resources, it is possible to prepare and finance a large and complex infrastructure project. That said, the size of the financing package under NT2 was possible because of a confluence of favorable factors that may not always be present in other country situations.
- Concession agreements that clearly define the relative roles and responsibilities of the government and the developers are critical in large infrastructure projects. This is particularly important in countries with limited human and financial capacity, which need to rely on private developers to undertake responsibilities the government is unable to meet. In future projects, a concession agreement that is more detailed, prepared earlier, and crafted with some participation by the World Bank should be considered.
- A decision framework is a constructive way of reaching agreement with the government on the broad principles of ultimate World Bank engagement in large infrastructure projects. For future projects, the decision framework could be used to reach more detailed agreements, with the objective of increasing the predictability of expectations, while still allowing flexibility in defined areas as project preparation proceeds. The deci-

sion framework could also be used to involve key participants other than the government.

- Arranging financing to match the dollar/local currency split of the revenue stream is worth replicating to the extent possible in large projects that have an expected revenue stream in multiple currencies.
- In poor countries, innovative financing of the government's equity can increase the overall returns of the government in private infrastructure projects.
- For large private sector infrastructure projects, World Bank procurement rules need to be flexibly applied and adjusted to realities on the ground, as was done in some instances in NT2. The standard procurement rules applied to public sector projects may not be appropriate for private sector projects.
- If one is to effectively manage exchanges of information on complex projects across a broad array of interested parties, communications must be transparent, positions well defined, and messages consistent; up-to-date information should be maintained on well-designed Web sites.
- The presence of a large and capable team is essential for the preparation of complex infrastructure projects. An elaborate structure of oversight and monitoring groups seems to be necessary to address the needs of such projects.

NT2 also revealed areas in which World Bank performance could be improved:

- The World Bank needs to do a better job of understanding the constraints under which the private sector works and to candidly explain to private partners up front any limitations in its ability to accommodate their concerns. It needs to ensure that staff members who are skilled at working with the private sector are assigned to private sector infrastructure projects. If necessary, such staff should be hired from the private sector.
- It is not enough to get the end-product right; the World Bank and other donors need to focus on the process of getting there. Improving process efficiency is critical. Early in the preparation process, the financial and other costs that have to be borne by the developers must be clearly spelled out and agreed to. The private sector needs more predictable budget and cost estimates up front; it has serious problems with open-ended commitments. Coordination between multiple experts and missions needs improvement, so that different messages are not conveyed to partners.

Ensuring the predictability of expectations and avoiding the perception of "shifting goalposts" is critical.

- The World Bank needs to define a clearer and more transparent policy for cost recovery of project preparation costs for high-profile, high-cost projects. The only current policy is articulated in the Board paper on enclave projects, which allows, in exceptional projects, the recovery of up to $0.5 million more than usual internal preparation costs. In cases such as NT2, for which the preparation costs are unusually high, it is reasonable for the World Bank to seek a more significant share of cost recovery. Developers may be willing to pay larger amounts, provided the policy is transparent and the level of possible fees is clearly indicated up front.

- The World Bank should consider whether processing efficiency might be improved by including a smaller number of participants (official agencies and banks). Alternatively, the official agencies could consider emulating the consortium approach used by banks, under which there are explicit understandings about allocating lead responsibilities among the participating banks for specific areas.

- It is important that in large and complex projects the information flow, particularly among partners, is managed to provide timely information in an easily digestible form.

- The World Bank needs to consider more carefully the balance between its financing role and the policy leverage it exercises, to reflect the fact that its use of policy leverage both imposes costs on and yields benefits for borrower and developers.

- In large, high-visibility, and contentious projects, the World Bank needs to strike a balance between the need for continuous senior management oversight and the need to maintain the authority of the team manager with respect to both internal and external players. It may be worth considering the development of explicit Bank-wide mechanisms to designate a few projects as corporate priorities. Such a designation should trigger an institutionally chosen core team, which is freed from other duties for an extended period and led by a senior staff member. Creation of such a team would not obviate the need for intensive senior management involvement, but it would curb the need for too much intervention by raising the comfort level of senior management. It would also address the problems of funding the high costs of project preparation, which need to be institutionally funded, and of team continuity, which became an issue in some aspects of NT2.

- Detailed risk identification early in the project preparation cycle and development of risk-mitigation measures to cover all risks will lead to a risk-avoidance strategy rather than an appropriate risk-management strategy. A more nuanced risk-management approach needs to be developed, as discussed next.

Improve the World Bank's project preparation strategy. For future large infrastructure projects, the World Bank may wish to address risk management in a two-stage decision process. At the first stage, early in the project cycle, the World Bank would decide in principle whether or not to fund the project. This decision could be based on an up-front assessment of risks and rewards and the practicality of mitigating risks to an acceptable level.

If positive, such a decision should be followed by a decision framework. This framework should extend beyond the broad principles of World Bank engagement and broad commitments by the government used in NT2. It should include a set of detailed (yet flexible), monitorable targets, anchored in a two- to three-year work program, supported by donor and government budgets, with work-sharing arrangements with financiers and partners. The multiyear work program could be adjusted annually to take account of changing circumstances.

The decision framework should be deepened and developed into a project framework. Building on the rationale of engineering credits, which the World Bank has used in the past to finance preparation of complex projects, such a project preparation framework and its associated costs could be submitted to the World Bank Board for approval. Using such a framework would help ensure better project preparation by identifying the substance and sequence of technical work and due diligence and ensuring proper funding and supervision of these activities. It would underpin these activities with transparency and provide a mechanism to enforce accountability of all players involved in project preparation. It would make coordination among donors more efficient. It would provide the framework for consultation and participation of all stakeholders and help underpin a constructive and continuous debate among them on the pros and cons of a large infrastructure project. It would also have the advantage of providing some signals from the World Bank's Board on the strength of its support for the project. At the second stage, such a framework, if implemented to the satisfaction of the World Bank, would lead to the World Bank's ultimate decision on involvement in the project.

This approach should provide more comfort to the government and private sector partners. It would signal interest by the World Bank earlier; establish transparent, measurable, and monitorable goalposts; and prompt the developers to commit resources to design safeguards sooner than was the case in NT2. It would also help create an environment in which the government would agree to jump-start capacity building earlier, at both the national and project level. For the World Bank, such an approach would reduce the risks of providing signals on its ultimate involvement too early, without having completed its due diligence.

In addition, the World Bank's institutional tendencies toward risk aversion in high-visibility cases need to be controlled by having senior management give strong signals to staff encouraging discussion of appropriate risk-management strategies during the various levels of review. Senior managers need to set a good example by demonstrating that they are willing to take carefully considered risks if the risk-reward trade-off makes it worthwhile to do so.

Improve the World Bank's capacity-building efforts. The challenge faced in NT2 was to build national capacity to mobilize financial partners, establish legal frameworks, and allocate risks in a manner that is conducive to macroeconomic and environmental stability. Although various efforts were made at building the capacity of weak Lao institutions, it proved difficult to strike the right balance between allowing the necessary time to develop local skills and capacities, which would delay project preparation, and the need to get the job done right and quickly.

This trade-off manifested itself in various ways. First, over the course of the project, NTPC was given an increasingly important role in designing and implementing environmental and social mitigation measures, for which capacity in the government agencies was limited; government agencies took on more of an oversight and regulatory function. Partly because the developer was instrumental in persuading the government to work with the World Bank, the government considered NTPC as the real broker in its relationship with the World Bank. The government relied extensively on advisors on various parts of the process, and the developers often identified and paid for them.

Second, very little effort was made to develop local expertise regarding the legal framework for private-public projects. Instead, as in the case of other, even more sophisticated borrowers, extensive use was made of international financial and legal advisors, in addition to Lao and Thai lawyers. The mandate given to the legal advisors by the World Bank in 1995 did not include any provision for training national staff. The Public Private Infrastructure Advisory Facility (PPIAF) agreement signed in early 2005, under which the government legal advisors worked, contained a small budget for capacity building.

Third, the World Bank played an extensive and continuous role in coordinating activities with other multilateral and bilateral official agencies. The government and NTPC no doubt benefited a great deal in the process of learning through doing and working with the World Bank. As the project was recast in the context of a development program—with complementary projects financed through additional instruments to address issues that lay beyond the scope of the developer's mandate—the government became more proactive in its dealings with the World Bank.

World Bank Institute staff in Lao PDR reported that there had been tremendous learning and capacity gains among a core group of staff on financial analysis; project finance; legal terms, conditions, and liabilities; contract risk; and the EGAT–PPA negotiations. In the absence of agreed measurement criteria, however, it is difficult to determine the significance of country staff perceptions. What types of capacity were built? At what scale? In what context? Would the Ministry of Energy and Mines be able to manage the entire process without substantial help from the international financial institutions in the future? Did the request for help from the World Bank reflect the government's need for funding for advisors or its need for technical help? Is the ministry now well positioned to deal with possible future contract failures or renegotiations?

Ministry of Industry staff noted that World Bank experts had been extensively involved in providing guidance in the contract design.[6] Financial and legal advisers financed by the IDA credits provided critical support to the government on the concession agreement and the PPA. World Bank staff were directly involved in providing support for Schedule 4 of the concession agreement, which deals with safeguards. In fact, Schedule 4 was reworked with the World Bank's full due diligence and review. A small group of government staff was already capable of contracting and managing international consultants. No significant additional in-house capacity was developed to deepen the skills beyond this group, although learning through involvement in the work no doubt occurred. In the future, it would be useful for the Ministry of Energy and Mines to think in terms of the types and range of technical capacity needed to take a memorandum of understanding through the project cycle to financial close without the assistance of the international financial institutions. Equally important, the ministry needs to focus on increasing its capacity to deal with possible renegotiations and contract failure and on broadening the expertise beyond a very small number of government officials.

The lack of baseline data on capacity indicators in NT2 hampers any meaningful attempt to measure changes during implementation and beyond. Some specific areas of useful inquiry on capacity should include a basic measurement scale for each of the skills areas required in complex project finance transactions, including those that can be contracted out and those that should be retained in-house, as well as some rough estimation of the capacity level at the start of preparation and at financial close and estimates of capacity needs during each year of the project. Means of addressing core capacity deficits (study tours, comprehensive project finance training, concession management training) should also be identified.

The larger learning issue for the World Bank is the extent to which a donor should assist a client in preparing complex concessions in small, low-capacity countries and what type of capacity development is appropriate to foster a sense of true ownership of contractual details during the process. The main lesson that emerges is that national capacity building should be an integral objective of large and complex projects—but only in countries with a number of large infrastructure projects in the pipeline, not in countries in which such possibilities are very limited.

Increasing the Replicability of NT2

Is the experience of NT2 replicable? Some participants expressed concern that the high standards applied and the high preparation costs may not be replicable in other large infrastructure projects that do not have the unusually favorable economics of NT2 and the involvement of a reputable developer with deep pockets. Within the World Bank, the intensive internal review mechanisms and the amount of World Bank management time spent on NT2 through the project oversight group and visits to Lao PDR by the managing director and the president of the World Bank may also be replicable for only a few high visibility projects.

With appropriate adjustments, however, the lessons of NT2 can be meaningfully applied in a number of large infrastructure projects. The proposed adjustments relate mainly to the World Bank's risk-management strategy and the efficiency of project management and internal processes. It would be desirable in future large infrastructure projects to focus up front on the key risks involved, to design mitigation measures for them, and to consciously leave other risks to be dealt with later, in consultation with public and private partners, as the situation develops. The two-step process for risk management and project preparation described in this chapter is worth trying.

Another major issue for the future, contemplated during NT2 prepartion, is whether, based on the NT2 experience, private partners would seek to involve the World Bank in other large infrastructure projects in East Asia or other regions. Private and public partners' perceptions of the World Bank are not uniform, but some indicated that they would prefer to fund large infrastructure projects in East Asia without the World Bank. Their hierarchy of preferences ranks private sector funding first; assistance from export credit agencies—and if necessary, IFC, MIGA, or ADB—second; and World Bank involvement last. The lesson the World Bank needs to draw from this is that there is a critical need to reduce the costs the private sector incurs for doing business with it. To do so, the institution needs to better understand the constraints under which the private sector works.

From the World Bank's point of view, the good news is that its hard work and high standards led to the successful introduction of Lao PDR to the private international markets and opened up possibilities for private developers to seriously consider large infrastructure projects in other low-income East Asian countries with weak creditworthiness. Preliminary proposals have already been made to EGAT for a number of additional cross-border energy projects for supply of power to Thailand, without the involvement of multilateral institutions.

Notes

1. The Government Letter of Implementation Policy (GLIP) document (found in Annex 1 to the NT2 Project Appraisal Document, Report No: 31764-LA, March 31, 2005) sets forth the Government's commitment to its reform program, focusing on elements critical to successful NT2 implementation and the achievement of the government's development objectives. In addition, the World Bank's overall NT2 package included two other operations: (a) the Lao Environment and Social (LEnS) project, which supports the strengthening of the management of environmental and social issues associated with the sustainable use of natural resources in Lao PDR, to enhance the quality of growth and reduce poverty, and (b) the Public Financial Management Strengthening Program (PFMSP), for support to revenue management and the establishment of targeted allocation arrangements for NT2

revenues. The World Bank also committed to supporting the Khammouane Development Project to enhance opportunities for villagers living near, but not within, the area impacted by the NT2 project.

2. The GLIP provides a framework and spells out commitments on the part of the Government of Lao PDR to (i) sustain policies and institutions developed within the NT2 project and (ii) extend them beyond the project to the wider government context.

3. It has been estimated that 40,000 people living along the Xe Bang Fai will be directly affected by the project. An additional 30,000 people along tributaries and hinterland villages in the basin of the Xe Bang Fai could also be adversely affected through reduced access to river fisheries.

4. Border prices are prices observed at the border for imports on a c.i.f. (cost, insurance, and freight) basis or for exports on a f.o.b. (free on board) basis.

5. Within the World Bank, economic appraisal of power projects requires integrating externalities to the extent feasible, by treating environmental and social costs (and benefits) like any other project costs (or benefits).

6. During the earlier years of NT2 project development, hydropower development came under the Ministry of Industry and Handicrafts. It is currently handled by the Ministry of Energy and Mines.

CHAPTER 4

Working with Stakeholders

Nazir Ahmad

The Nam Theun 2 (NT2) project in Lao PDR was prepared in fits and starts over the course of more than a decade. During this period, the roster of stakeholders—both official and unofficial—expanded and contracted, and their roles, relationships, and mutual expectations evolved. These changes stemmed both from greater familiarity with one another's objectives and constraints over time, and the fact that the consensus on what constitutes best practices for large infrastructure projects such as NT2 continues to evolve.

The initial impetus for developing this project on the Nam Theun River came from the private sector in the early to mid-1990s. The East Asian financial crisis in 1997 and the decrease in Thailand's demand for power stalled the project until 1999. The project took on a new life in 2001, with some changes in the developer group and a markedly different international environment for large hydropower projects. Nine multilaterals, bilaterals, and export credit agencies provided direct loans, guarantees, and funding for the government's equity contribution.[1]

With the resolution of the Asian financial crisis, the World Bank reengaged in the project in a serious manner. A management mission in August 2001 led by the World Bank country director for Lao PDR restarted the discussion in an environment of greater concern for environmental and social safeguards and greater risk sensitivity on the part of senior World Bank management in light of the controversies associated with major infrastructure projects elsewhere.

By 2001, it was no longer sufficient for NT2 to be a technically sound hydropower project: it had to be set in the overall development framework of Lao PDR, and the revenues generated by the project had to be used for poverty reduction. The decision framework prepared by the World Bank and agreed with the government in 2001 laid out these revised principles.

Two other significant features were introduced in project preparation. First, a project oversight group, chaired by the World Bank regional vice president, was established. It periodically convened all key directors to review, coordinate, and manage progress under NT2. Second, the communications team in the East Asia and Pacific Region was engaged to manage the complex communications process involved with the proposed project.

For the lessons of NT2 to be credible, the World Bank needs to continue to facilitate evidence-based research, dialogue, and debate across a wide spectrum of interested parties.

Soliciting the Views of People Affected by the Project: From Monologue to Dialogue

The initial engagement with local populations had two objectives: to identify issues salient to the technical design of the hydropower project and to demonstrate to nongovernmental organizations (NGOs), potential investors, and donors that the population in the project areas was supportive of the project. The initial scope of such consultations was focused on the plateau and, to a very limited extent, the protected area.

Few infrastructure projects have adequately taken into account the second-order effects of project-related uncertainties on the affected populations. The possibility of being targeted for resettlement is likely to set off a course of gradual divestment of assets. As the International Advisory Group notes, this dynamic has important bearings on what constitutes a baseline for project-affected people. If the baseline is conducted after their assets and livelihood prospects have been devalued, the project-affected populations risk receiving a smaller share of the economic rents accruing from the project than they deserve. Having an accurate baseline in place early on is thus essential.

CARE and subsequently, in 1997–98, the International Union for Conservation of Nature (IUCN) were engaged to assist the government in the consultation process. A basic socioeconomic baseline was developed in 1996. IUCN experts held numerous meetings in various villages, but the focus was largely on conservation research, with some complementary sociocultural information gathering.

The early consultations were characterized by a narrow technical focus. The initial idea of consultations was to transmit information rather than to engage in dialogue. The "consultations" were actually intended to convey to the population the developer's and government's story regarding the benefits of the project. They did not solicit or facilitate the surfacing of uncomfortable questions or opinions on the part of villagers. (It is interesting to note that the Lao term for consultations translates as "public relations," not "public consultations.")

Concerns about how consultations had been conducted and the extent to which they had effectively gathered and synthesized concerns and options became salient in 2002–03. During visits to the plateau, World Bank staff became convinced that the local population had been told about the benefits but not the costs of the project. To gain support from the World Bank, the project needed legitimacy, which could be attained only by forthrightly sharing and discussing the pros and cons of the project with the local population and seeking their input on appropriate design and mitigation approaches. Country team management signaled that the quality of local consultations would be an important determinant of support from the Board and other influential stakeholders. Although Lao PDR was perceived as a closed political system, the World Bank's experience with the Poverty Reduction Strategy Paper (PRSP) consultations in Lao PDR and neighboring Vietnam suggested that if skillfully facilitated, consultations in a "closed" system could yield surprising and substantial feedback on a proposed project.

The Report of the World Commission on Dams, as well as the World Bank's own policies, emphasized the critical role of local consultations during the design phase. Several skeptical NGOs accused the World Bank and the project developer of neglecting to listen to the voices or consider the interests of the affected populations. The inadequacies of resettlement practices in other hydropower projects in Southeast Asia also loomed large in the background. World Bank staff themselves returned from site visits concerned that low-quality and insufficient input from the affected populations would result in poor design of resettlement and compensation programs.

In 2003 the World Bank commissioned a review of the local consultation process used for NT2 up to that point. The analysis found significant deficiencies. The same year the World Bank determined that the Indigenous Peoples Policy would apply to NT2, reinforcing the need for the conduct of a quality consultations process. The lack of meaningful consultations would preclude adherence to the safeguards, which would be a serious impediment to the project achieving the approval of the World Bank and other financial institutions involved in it. In view of these findings, the World Bank determined that the local consultation process had to be thoroughly redesigned to meet the highest international standards.

A new consultation methodology was developed for the World Bank by a well-respected Lao-speaking Thai social scientist, who advised the Bank that the consultations needed to invite full and unscripted feedback. This could be achieved through a consultation process that involved an approach of "talk less, listen more." Such an approach would require clear intentions, skill, humility, and a disciplined process to mitigate the risk of particularly strong voices dominating discussions. It was recognized that honest feedback would be possible only by tailoring the consultation to the considerable ethnic and biophysical diversity of the areas affected by the project. Doing so required segmenting participants into culturally and ethnically compatible groups.

Furthermore, to facilitate participation in areas in which large proportions of the population are illiterate, pictorial posters and icons, tailored to the three areas affected (watershed, resettlement, and downstream), were developed to communicate key concepts and issues. The posters highlighted the area-specific issues that had emerged in trial consultations, so that each village could use them to jumpstart its discussion and then elaborate on its own views and implications. The successful use of these pictorials demonstrated that difficult issues were possible to unpack. As an added precaution, to ensure that the consultation process was robust and meaningful and would stand up to international scrutiny, the international financial institutions engaged a well-respected international social anthropologist with expertise on Lao PDR. In addition to conducting the initial study that documented the severe shortcomings of the earlier consultations, the anthropologist monitored the subsequent consultations and verified that they took place in an open and noncoercive manner.[2]

The consultation process was designed to allow small group interactions, facilitated by individuals from the community who were trained as "village facilitators." Discussion groups were organized around demographic attributes such as age and gender. (An attempt was made to create a group made up exclusively of the poorest segments of the village population, but doing so proved difficult and the effort was abandoned.) In addition, other logical groupings, such as organized community groups (for example, the local branch of the official women's association) were also represented in the consultations.

Government participation in the consultations primarily involved local government officials, who had both stronger ties to the region and greater accountability for the project's outcome than did representatives from the capital, whose involvement was more sporadic. The government was initially nervous about the consultations, which were new to Lao PDR, but its apprehensiveness gradually dissipated as it became evident that the consultations would involve, not bypass, them. It was important for the government to recognize that the consultations would be well managed to elicit the needed information and report on it in a sensitive but constructive way to inform project design while respecting the political and cultural ways of the country. Many people in government were themselves from the general project area and genuinely wanted to craft a just mitigation policy for the resettled population; they were open to new ideas and to listening, as long as doing so did not upset the basic tenets of government. The consultation methodology encouraged a broad array of opinions to be heard and taken into account while ensuring that influential voices did not dominate the discussions.

Although imperfect, the incorporation of feedback from the consultations about NT2 into project design and approach is widely viewed as having been more substantive than in any other large, multidonor financed infrastructure project in Lao PDR. The initial consultations (described earlier), were critical in changing initial resettlement plans. For example, the technical experts initially proposed that the displaced population be resettled halfway down the plateau, where the soil quality is better than elsewhere in the area. Consultations revealed the deep concerns of villagers, who wanted to stay on top of the plateau for spiritual and social reasons. Accommodating their desires complicated the project design, but it also forced creative thinking about designing a far more robust livelihood program.

When building on the information drawn from the consultations, sometimes the response was less than adequate. For example, the livelihood options menu developed was technically sophisticated and sometimes overwhelming to affected populations. Also, the psychological impacts of shifting from extensive to intensive cultivation, or of raising livestock in pens rather than grazing, may have been underestimated. The quality of the local consultations would have been higher if some of the critical analysis generated internationally had been translated and disseminated to the affected populations, perhaps through pictorials or other modalities tailored to be most effective in reaching the relevant audience (many of whom lack reading skills). This was only done in the more recent rounds of local consultations.

Given that the lifestyles of the affected populations would change dramatically as a consequence of the project, archiving their raw input—the set of initial aspirations and concerns—from the 200 villages in which consultations were conducted would have retained valuable baseline information. A reconsideration of the approach regarding how the content of local consultations should be categorized, utilized, and archived might be useful.

Several lessons about consultation emerge from this experience:

- Begin local consultations as early as possible in the project development process, with adequate baseline data collected beforehand to best capture the views, concerns, and conditions of people affected by the project.
- Fully explore the impact of the project with the affected populations. Brainstorm with them on the value of the project and their doubts or concerns. Do so in a language (or pictorials) they understand, and ensure that the lack of formal education is not a barrier to raising questions and providing input.
- Involve government officials (such as local government officials living in or near the affected villages) in the consultation process, so that the government does not feel sidelined and learns to appreciate the value of consultation techniques.
- Establish and enforce clear ground rules to prevent authority figures from dominating discussions.
- Explicitly discuss compensation and grievance options. Do not make assumptions about what is valuable to people; ask them what matters.
- As appropriate, segment the affected populations based on issues, characteristics, and concerns and tailor consultation approaches, materials, or both for the affected areas.
- Expect variations in expressed concerns by geography and cultural affiliation, and do not lose the distinctions during the synthesis of findings.
- Build a cadre of local facilitators, and ensure that they are trained and empowered to serve as an ongoing and credible resource to the community.
- Engage an independent monitor to ensure the effectiveness of local consultations.

Working with the Government:
Deepening Trust and Cultivating Confidence

Before 1999 the government's role in the project was limited. It trusted and enjoyed cordial relations with the developer, Nam Theun 2 Power Company (NTPC, formerly NTEC) and signed off on the key principles guiding the project. The government left the developer to manage most aspects of project preparation, particularly in aspects in which it lacked the full capacity to handle the activities itself. Because NTPC was critically involved in persuading the government to partner with the World Bank, for a long time the government viewed it as the real broker of its relationship with the Bank. The government relied extensively on external advisors, who were often identified and paid for by NTPC. Such high reliance on NTPC may have slowed the growth of government capacity, which the World Bank should have done more to develop.

This reliance on the developer worked reasonably well as long as NT2 was seen as a discrete hydropower project. After NT2 was reframed as an engine for national development with major implications for national revenue management, environmental policy, and community development, the government's active leadership became more important.

During project preparation, particularly before 2001, trust between the government and the World Bank was limited. Many in the government's political leadership were concerned about what they perceived as the politically intrusive nature of the World Bank's tendency to impose conditions. Lao political leaders admired the economic prosperity of their neighbors but were concerned about potential social disruption. Government officials believed that the World Bank's demands were excessive and that it was using a single project to extract substantial commitments. They were also concerned about the government's human and organizational absorptive capacity and the drain of human resources from other efforts. As one key official stated, "The cost of being a model project was too high, and we paid that price. Not again." For their part, many people at the World Bank (and in some shareholder governments) saw Lao PDR as a closed system, which they feared might make successful collaboration difficult.

Starting in late 2001, and particularly in the two years leading up to Board approval of NT2, there was a significant increase in both the role and active leadership of the government. As a result of the preparation of the PRSP and the appraisal of several projects (including the Financial

Management Adjustment Credit [FMAC]), the World Bank and the government established mutual confidence and trust. The government's agreement to place a moratorium on logging—and its enforcement of the moratorium—impressed donors. Negotiation of the revenue-management arrangements in the two-track approach (see chapter 2) convinced the government that the World Bank would not insist on an unreasonable ring-fencing of revenues, and a mutually satisfactory arrangement was reached. Perhaps as significant in building trust was the World Bank's support after the sudden withdrawal in 2003 (for reasons unrelated to NT2) of Electricité de France (EdF) from the developer consortium, which required an intensive campaign at the highest levels of the government to reinvolve it in the project.

Several lessons about working with the government emerged from the NT2 project:

- Start with a quick assessment of the fundamental objectives of all key stakeholders, along with their organizational arrangements and most pressing relevant capacity constraints, to avoid unforeseen conflicts down the road.
- Be clear with the government and counterparts about what requirements, provisions, and standards are nonnegotiable, and communicate the reasons they are in the best interest of the country's development, drawing on the World Bank's relevant experience elsewhere, so that there is common understanding about what is at stake and what is expected and needed.
- Develop a shared understanding of risks and rewards, and help ensure that the counterparts receive the best information to help make their decisions in managing the delicate balance.
- Conduct a power, influence, and capability mapping of key stakeholders and identify modes of engagement that can simultaneously build the trust and competence of the principal counterpart organizations.
- Accept that some conditionalities may be unpalatable. In such instances, explain the rationale and help the client develop the technical skills to meet these requirements, if it demonstrates the political will to do so.
- Where feasible, build an extended network of influential agents (government officials, academics, media, business leaders, and so forth) who can serve as channels for reinforcing the political will for reforms.

Working with the Developer: Clarifying Objectives, Overcoming Differences, and Improving Project Outcomes

Relations between the World Bank and the developer were strained at times, because of the different—and sometimes conflicting—interests of the two parties. The World Bank's central concern was the impact of the project on development in Lao PDR, including its environmental and social effects; the developers were understandably interested in finishing the project quickly and profitably, given pressures from their shareholders. Not sensing a firm commitment from the World Bank to go ahead with the project, the developers felt that they were being asked to absorb expenses that they were uncertain about being able to recoup. The developer wanted to reserve some contingency funds for future requirements for environmental and social remediation; the World Bank insisted that NTPC cost and allocate known resettlement and remediation costs ex ante, with the contingency reserves set aside only for unknown costs.

Some World Bank staff perceived NTPC as occasionally reticent about cooperation, especially regarding the conduct of downstream studies and the provision of environmental and social remediation. The process of getting to closure was contentious, but the potential to reach the desired development outcomes was improved by diligently working through differences. In the future, a project framework agreement, spelling out the roles and responsibilities of each party, should be developed at the outset. It should then be reviewed, steered, and monitored by major stakeholders on a periodic basis.

To some extent, NT2 benefited from geopolitical considerations. Although NTPC is a private company, its key investor, EdF, is a French public sector enterprise, and the principal customer for the power is a Thai government enterprise. Financial and geopolitical considerations converged to keep the developer and customer committed to NT2 throughout the turbulence of project preparation. The same degree of commitment and staying power may not have been achievable with a purely private sector investor.

Several lessons about working with the developer emerge from NT2:

- Establish a strong project management role to manage expectations, work demands, and communications with key counterparts.
- Assign single points of contact in the World Bank (by issue, counterpart, or both) with clear expectation that this person (or persons) will be responsible for consulting the right people in the Bank and facilitating

efficient communications. These liaisons should serve as facilitators rather than as gatekeepers of communications.

- Create an internal project management Web site on which all project preparation activities and accountabilities are recorded, updated, and displayed. This would minimize confusion and incoherence.
- Limit the size of missions when feasible, taking into account the response and hosting capacity of the government and developer.
- Identify up front the client capacity needs that can be addressed in the course of project preparation, and seek avenues to provide such learning opportunities to client personnel, e.g., learning-by-doing.
- Recognize that forging ahead using the developers' capacity to cover areas in which the government faces capacity constraints, without the government's active involvement in the activities to help build its capacity and prepare for the eventual handover of responsibilities, perpetuates capacity deficits and can risk implementation quality in the long run.

Working with NGOs Opposed to the Project: Forging a Path to Constructive Engagement

NT2 attracted criticisms from the outset. Most vocal were activist NGOs that fundamentally dislike dam projects based on the adverse environmental and human consequences of many other projects they have witnessed. Over the years, it became increasingly necessary for the World Bank to develop a strategy to manage communications more proactively and constructively so that balanced, factual information was made available to all stakeholders and the World Bank's reputation was protected from unfair accusations. Communications would become a strategic lever to facilitate the debate and make it constructive; however, this was more easily said than done. On the one hand, the institution may have missed opportunities for real dialogue and learning from critics, especially during the later phase of project preparation. On the other hand, the efforts needed to try to satisfy critics who would not be swayed from their opposition to the project, no matter what arguments were presented, could have reduced the benefits offered by engagement with more constructive partners. And sadly, the extent, richness, and fervor of debate among World Bank staff over whether to proceed with the project was largely invisible to its most vocal critics, who might have been more receptive to constructive dialogue with the World Bank if they had experienced greater exposure to the robust debate occurring inside the organization.

It is interesting to note that at one point near the end of the project preparation cycle, the World Bank challenged some of the critics of the project to specify the circumstances under which they would support a hydropower project. No responses were submitted. Questions such as these were dismissed as rhetorical and "unserious," making it difficult to engage in constructive debate. The critics complained that the World Bank was philosophically predisposed to large hydropower projects and therefore analyzed only alternative sites or designs for an NT2 dam, not alternatives to dams.[3] At a press briefing in March 2005, project opponents were asked what kind of alternatives to NT2 they would propose to address Lao PDR's poverty and environmental degradation. One NGO responded that as the World Bank was building the dam, it was up to the World Bank to devise the alternatives. This comment illustrates the challenge of achieving constructive debate in this arena. At the same time, many criticisms of the World Bank were helpful. Several Bank staff interviewed noted that by pointing out problems that might otherwise have been overlooked, the critics did help strengthen thinking about project issues—and a number of questions posed by critics of NT2 merited ongoing attention, including during project implementation:

- How would a government with limited capacity manage the complex resettlement envisioned in the plan?
- Given that the World Bank typically carries out project oversight through site visits rather than a presence on the ground, how would it make sure that the rights of the affected populations were safeguarded?
- Given the weak capacity of the government, much of the resettlement work might be carried out by the developer. How appropriate is it to give the developer responsibility for ensuring that social and environmental impacts are fully addressed? Does the developer have the skills and track record to do so?
- Given what critics see as a track record of "broken promises" and the "environmentally ruinous legacy" of hydropower projects worldwide, are the risk mitigation steps taken for NT2 sufficient to justify the confidence that NT2 will be different?

In one way or another, the World Bank endeavored to address these questions during preparation efforts, with ongoing efforts carrying on into implementation. Throughout the project preparation process, the World

Bank's external relations staff in East Asia tried to be responsive to the critics. Written correspondence was addressed as thoroughly as possible. Yet, opponents of the project give the World Bank little credit for its efforts to address inquiries and challenges.

Given these difficulties, how can the World Bank constructively interact with NGOs that oppose its projects? Is there reason to believe that, in the future, the preparation of controversial and complex projects will also benefit from being challenged by skeptics and critics? During the preparation of NT2, the communications strategy was very effective in some ways (such as ensuring factual and analytical information was publicly available), less so in others. Some participants found that the World Bank did not effectively incorporate or learn from the views of tough critics; mastering how to do so without surrendering to or marginalizing them remains a challenge.

Once a controversial project is approved, it is tempting to write off and ignore project critics. Instead, the World Bank should proactively find ways to engage them during the implementation process. The period of implementation provides a tangible basis to advance a common understanding based on evidence unfolding on the ground rather than preconceived and potentially outdated notions held by either party. Given the good quality and large quantity of due diligence and analytical work on NT2, the potential for productive, evidence-based learning and consensus building is significant and should be exploited. NT2 implementation can be a learning lab for further identifying do's and don't's of hydropower and other infrastructure projects.

Learning from—and with—critics is not enough; the World Bank also needs to understand the ideological and political context in which their views are formed. NGO opponents to hydropower are not a monolithic group. Some opponents were willing to stretch and misstate the facts to suit their message.[4] Other respected NGOs saw value in the project but were pressured or convinced to ultimately oppose NT2. How much independence does the undecided middle truly enjoy, and how can the World Bank foster such independence? Complex projects like NT2 often chart new territory; unfriendly and seemingly "unfair" criticism can be helpful in triggering the World Bank to more deeply reexamine its assumptions and predispositions.

Many recommendations emerge from analyzing the World Bank's experience with NGOs:

- Adopt a proactive communications strategy from the beginning, and ensure that meaningful, accurate, accessible, and timely information is available to all stakeholders. This is particularly important on controversial, high-profile projects.

- Segment and carefully map out the positions and concerns of each group of stakeholders as they see it, and customize the communications approach for each.
- Avoid letting critics control the debate, but do not marginalize or trivialize them.
- Engage the middle ground, and do not focus only on the extreme elements. The harshest critics will flag what could go wrong; those occupying the middle ground are more likely to identify what can be done to avoid problems.
- Develop specific but flexible guidelines that help World Bank staff differentiate between groups that have genuine concerns from those that are just trying to stall or prevent a project.
- Have a system in place to catalogue and evaluate criticisms, incorporate legitimate concerns into project design, and communicate the World Bank's response and commitments with evidence and milestones.
- Multiple approaches are needed to provide information and overcome access challenges. Use Web sites, email, and other media platforms to demonstrate the World Bank's transparency. Use public information space to respond to specific concerns regarding project design or benefits.
- Go beyond ensuring timeliness and accessibility. Ensure that all materials put in the public domain are clearly presented and, to the extent possible, jargon-free. Establish quality standards and utilize user feedback systematically.
- Provide communications training to key management and technical staff so that they can be effective spokespeople for the World Bank. Also train them to be better listeners.
- Anticipate negative press, and manage expectations and reactions of senior managers to criticism.
- Clearly communicate the World Bank's decision basis (in the case of NT2, the "decision framework") to all constituencies and stakeholders, so that they know the context within which the Bank's decision making is advancing.
- Jointly with the client, other donors, and key stakeholders—including project affected persons and water users—plan and execute the communications strategy, which could include presentations, interviews, and newspaper opinion pieces.
- Continue a systematic communications program during implementation, maintaining a healthy balance between defending the World Bank and listening for problems and bringing them to the attention of the Bank and the client.

- Ensure targeted communication is culturally sensitive in language and form to avoid swamping stakeholders with information they cannot process.

Engaging Stakeholders through International Workshops: Inviting Debate and Addressing Concerns

In 2004, the World Bank and its partner agencies organized international workshops in Vientiane, Bangkok, Paris, Tokyo, and Washington, DC, that included representatives of the government, other financial institutions, legislators, the private sector, the media, and NGOs. These workshops presented a forum for informed debate about the project, providing feedback to the government and NTPC before they finalized the safeguard documents and to the international financial institutions in considering support for the project. The workshops were held to ensure that the project's objectives, potential benefits, and impacts were shared, discussed, and well understood not only within Lao PDR but also more broadly among international civil society. The government was in the lead in these exchanges; donors and NTPC played supporting roles. At each of the workshops, an independent facilitator (engaged by the World Bank) sought to maintain objectivity and fairness. Reviews of the transcripts indicate that those who attended the sessions were not constrained in terms of the views they expressed.

Government officials had been hesitant about holding these workshops, fearing multifaceted and relatively unscripted public dialogue and potential public challenges by NGOs and Lao expatriate groups. As the workshops unfolded, however, officials appreciated the value of such engagement, both in explaining the project and in introducing Lao PDR to the outside world on the government's terms. The workshops were also successful in demonstrating the willingness of the government and the World Bank to engage with critics of the project.

Although the workshops were held too late to fundamentally affect technical infrastructure design choices, the consultations provided considerable opportunity for opponents to voice their views on social and environmental aspects. Some critics, concerned that their appearance at the workshop might be misconstrued as support for the project (despite the World Bank's public assurances to the contrary), made use of the opportunity to emphasize that they were not there to endorse the project.

Critics pointed out that the materials were not translated and posted sufficiently in advance. Some accused the World Bank of purposefully doing so to avoid scrutiny; in fact, the delays were caused by, inter alia, the strong tendency of Bank staff not to publish analysis without rigorous internal vetting on its quality.

Stakeholders also complained that the technical presentations and reports were too long and too technical. The technical aspects of project work are never easy to communicate in lay terms, but more could have been done in this regard. Given the scrutiny surrounding project preparation, proponents and opponents of the project were perceived to be only too ready to selectively seize the data that would support their respective positions. This perception made the technical experts particularly unwilling to disseminate their work in progress.

Many workshop participants were active critics of the project and they appropriated most of the airtime. The format of the international workshops thus allowed expression but did not permit true dialogue in a consistent manner—or actively help proponents, opponents, and those in the middle find common ground. Opponents in certain locations came with entrenched positions on certain issues. In this context, the willingness of government officials to provide unscripted answers and to entertain a range of politically hostile comments and questions was viewed as exceptional. At the end of the day, government officials nevertheless felt that they had had no chance to have a genuine dialogue with opponents, whose minds were already made up.

Several lessons about the value of international workshops emerged from this experience. The convening of international workshops should not become the modus operandi for all infrastructure projects. Such workshops are needed only for projects that face strong international concern from a diversity of stakeholders including governments, civil society organizations, and/or nongovernmental organizations or projects in which the support of a broad range of stakeholders is critical to optimal project design.

If international consultations are held, organizers should consider the following recommendations:

- Maintain open doors to proponents, opponents, and undecideds, and solicit the participation of individuals and groups representing diverse viewpoints.
- Provide background materials in forms that are accessible and comprehensible, and make them available early enough before the workshop that participants have time to review them.
- Design workshops so that they provide the opportunity for a variety of voices to be heard and limit the possibility for dominance by any one

perspective; help attendees (including World Bank staff) demonstrate that they have truly listened to various and opposing points of view. Provide an explanation of how the issues raised will be addressed.

- Enlist an independent moderator, and develop a facilitation process that focuses on joint brainstorming of problem identification and potential solutions.
- Use facilitation techniques that force participants to question their preconceived assumptions and assertions.
- Provide timely follow-up reports, including specific responses to specific inputs.
- Conduct formal evaluations to determine the efficacy of the design and conduct of consultations.

The international workshops were only one component of the multifaceted communications strategy adopted by the World Bank. The task of managing external perceptions and conducting substantive investigations into project issues was effectively shared between external relations and project staff. The team understood that civil society is not a monolithic entity and that it was risky to pay attention only to the loudest and most sensational while neglecting the "undecided middle."

To guide its work, an external relations team created a matrix of key stakeholders and their respective positions. The intended strategy was to be open about the dilemmas in World Bank decision making while also acknowledging that all major infrastructure projects had both potentially positive and adverse effects. A Web site was launched that posted technical studies and a variety of official documents. Several independent observers have praised the World Bank for being more forthcoming than usual but noted that the documents were frequently released late and were long and too technical for outsiders.

Effects of the World Bank's Internal Organization and Culture on Stakeholder Relations

Some organizational features of the World Bank made NT2 difficult to prepare. The multisectoral nature of the project design and the applicability of all 10 environmental and social safeguard policies led to coordination issues. The government and the developers found the World Bank's decision-making mechanisms diffuse and unpredictable, and they felt that the goalposts shifted during project preparation, leading to frustration with the World Bank's processes. To compound matters, frequent discussions of risk and "deal breakers" at project oversight group meetings, although necessary and useful, may have had the unintended consequence of making the World Bank overly risk averse by keeping the full range of risks prominently on the radar and not distinguishing adequately between the serious and not-so-serious risks. The World Bank's relationships with official agencies seemed to have worked better than with the private partners: both the World Bank and the Asian Development Bank (ADB) view their experience as an outstanding example of joint work.

A number of steps could have reduced the sense of frustration felt by the government and the developers:

- More centralized project management could have facilitated and coordinated information requests from sectoral experts.
- A clearer master plan of studies, jointly developed in advance, would have allowed all partners to take greater ownership of the studies and make better use of their results.
- Clarifying priorities and requirements up front, with some sort of ranking of proposed studies against different levels of budget availability and time-frames, would have been useful to the developers and government so they could better allocate their resources to meet the demands.
- Encouraging the developer to establish a small team to coordinate multiple studies would have improved quality and reduced costs. NTPC hired many consultants of variable quality, resulting in high transaction and review costs.

From the outset, senior World Bank staff clearly stated that the final decision on Bank support of NT2 would rest with the Board, as it always does, and that NT2 should expect considerable scrutiny from the Board even if the project was well prepared and management recommended approval. Preparations for the Board involved the usual collection of World Bank staff, government representatives, and advocacy groups (which have a history of lobbying the World Bank's managers and Board members).

Several recommendations about the World Bank's internal processes and culture emerge from NT2:

- Create a project preparation framework and roadmap at the outset of complex infrastructure projects, delineating roles, responsibilities, and dependencies of different parties. Use the preparation framework as a basis for allocating and negotiating responsibilities among parties, maintaining efficiency and alignment during preparation.

- Establish an explicit and integrated decision process for determining requirements for analytical studies, describing the rationale, necessity, and priority of the study; the intended audience and dissemination approach; the decision relevance and time frame; and the quality standards and expectations, including consultant qualifications and knowledge transfer expectations.
- Reduce "legacy blindness" by holding open discussions on how previous project experiences may be inadvertently shaping expectations and fears regarding the current project, and identify ways in which the current project is similar to and different from previous efforts. Acknowledge earlier deficiencies, but test whether they are inevitable in the context of the new project.
- On major controversial and high-profile projects, emphasize that the Board is the final arbiter of World Bank support.
- Track Board concerns in a systematic way, and use communications management tools to ensure that its concerns and questions are effectively and accurately addressed. In the case of NT2, the concerns and information requests of individual Executive Directors were meticulously tracked and responded to in a timely fashion.
- Ensure that parties trying to influence the Board have accurate information.
- Use the prelude to the Board decision as leverage for encouraging clients to adopt good policies.

Notes

1. Multilateral institutions included the World Bank (represented by the International Development Association [IDA] and the Multilateral Insurance Guaranty Agency [MIGA]) and the Asian Development Bank; bilateral institutions included Agence Française du Développement/Proparco, the Nordic Investment Bank, and the European Investment Bank; export credit agencies included Coface, Exportkreditnamnden, the Guarantee Institute for Export Credits, and the Export-Import Bank of Thailand.
2. One unforeseen cultural barrier that proved impossible to overcome was the lack of a cultural conception of the future among a small segment of the local population. The facilitator was unable to devise a way to communicate the longer-term consequences of the project (the central element of the discussions) with this population segment.
3. In fact, the World Bank examined broad alternatives (see chapter 2).
4. The rapid response to blatant inaccuracies and accusations during NT2 was unprecedented in the World Bank's recent experience. Such rapid response was essential in protecting the World Bank's reputation.

CHAPTER 5

The Communications Challenge

Peter Stephens

Without effective and open communication, the Nam Theun 2 (NT2) project could not have been brought to fruition. A number of the project stakeholders helped make this possible. Some faced steep learning curves. Others, like the World Bank, had to overcome the legacy of past failures. In the event, key stakeholders got their act together in a remarkable way. This chapter focuses on how the World Bank met the communications challenge. The analysis of this important component of the project would certainly benefit from similar "lessons learned" exercises by all other parties involved.

From the earliest days, the World Bank's communications team was fully involved. At critical times in the course of considering—and later preparing—the project, the communications team played a major role in ensuring that the World Bank's position was accurately portrayed and that Bank staff were aware of and understood the many concerns expressed by informed observers outside the World Bank. The team was not doing all the communicating, of course. The whole project team was involved, directly or indirectly, in doing so. The World Bank's actions—how it worked with others, the quality of its technical work—also communicated loudly. The communications team played a lead role at times, an advisory role at others, and sometimes a supporting or coordinating role.

The contributions of Jill Wilkins, Melissa Fossberg, Kimberly Versak, Cristina Mejia, and Pamornrat Tansanguanwong are gratefully acknowledged.

The Purpose of Communications

In many operations, the role of communications is never defined. As a result, communications often becomes a passive public relations operation or a reactive mechanism used to respond to public attacks.

In many earlier projects involving the World Bank, public criticism had forced the Bank team (often made up of economists, lawyers, financial specialists, engineers, and social scientists) to drop what they were doing and defend their position. This represented a signal failure of communications support. Just as communications specialists should not take the lead in designing bridges or drafting resettlement plans, it makes little sense for economists or engineers or lawyers to drive the communications strategy. But this is what had happened many times in the past, with all the attendant negative outcomes one would expect.

Early on in the World Bank's consideration of NT2, the core communications team set a simple goal: to create the space for all members of the team to do what they were there to do, while providing the necessary inputs to and support on communications issues. The two components—operations and communications—must go hand in hand.

Rules of the Game

To accomplish this goal, the World Bank team developed equally simple "rules of conduct" for the project. The most important of these was transparency—meaning that the Bank would communicate the project as it was, not "spin" it. The team was confident in proposing that because the technical and operational side of the team was of the highest quality. The communications specialists proposed—and the rest of the project team agreed, albeit nervously—that information would work either for the Bank or against it; and that it was important to ensure that the Bank could confidently disclose and discuss every aspect of its efforts. The Bank wanted to be open about what it knew and what it did not know, about mistakes made and problems encountered. The Bank believed that if it released all the relevant information that was legally permissible and responded to inquiries quickly and openly, it would allow people to understand the project for themselves.

Transparency works both ways, of course. It was equally important that the World Bank team be open to reading and hearing views, questions, and criticisms that it might find ill informed, disagreeable, and upsetting; and that it was able to discuss the project in full knowledge of all points of view.

At the outset, there were many sharply differing views within the World Bank about NT2, with the intensity of debate at least equaling that outside the institution. Whether it was concern over the quality of resettlement plans, illegal logging, or weaknesses in some of the early consultations, the debate was open and disagreement was encouraged. World Bank management made clear that it welcomed contrary views and difficult discussions and early in the project's consideration, organized a debate in which those who were known to favor the project were asked to attack it and those who were thought to oppose it were asked to speak in favor of it. It was a remarkable exercise, lasting four hours and enabling all sides to raise awkward issues and offer explanations. After that debate, the tone of openness and trust was clearly established; and throughout project preparation, World Bank management continued to emphasize the value of open communications. This sort of leadership made it possible for all members of the team to do their jobs. Without it, roles would have become blurred, people would have whispered in corridors, and the project team would not have functioned as a team.

A second principle was that the World Bank would define itself, internally and externally. The first step was to know exactly where the institution stood. In meetings of the NT2 project team, the communications group would present a slide on "where we stand" or "the message," using words that could be agreed on as a clear statement of the Bank's position. An early version of this statement said:

> The World Bank understands that the Nam Theun 2 project offers a real opportunity for Laos to earn money—but it also poses serious risks. That is why we are working with the government of Laos, the developer, with civil society groups and independent consultants to see if, on balance, this is the best thing for Laos. If it is, we will support it. If it isn't, we won't.

A later version read:

> The Nam Theun 2 project could provide a long-term source of income to pay for improved social services and infrastructure in Lao PDR, one of the world's poorest countries. The project also offers a chance to help the country improve the way it manages basic services, such as taxation, economic management, the power system and environmental protection. But it is a big project, and it entails

considerable risk. It also triggers all 10 of the World Bank's safeguard policies. The Bank would like to support the project, to benefit the people of Lao PDR, but is moving ahead cautiously so that, as far as possible, the risks are managed.

The shift from neutrality in the first statement to a conditional "would like to support the project" may seem slight, but it was important in capturing and accurately reflecting the sense of the team and the World Bank as a whole. If 40 people sitting around a table had slightly different ideas about where the Bank stood, discussion about next steps or tactics would lead only to confusion. It would also lead to confusion externally, because 40 people would each explain the Bank's position differently, reflecting their own biases or views. To be consistent externally, the Bank first had to be consistent internally.

Externally, the World Bank was determined that no other group would define its role or thinking. This also became a key element of the communications work. For example, the Bank insisted that NT2 be referred to as a "proposal" or "proposed project" rather than simply as a "project"—unless and until the Bank decided to support the project. This small point had major implications and prevented critics from talking about NT2 as a World Bank project before the Bank had decided to support it. Similarly, when critics wrote inaccurately about NT2 or the World Bank's position, the Bank wrote to them or the outlet in which their remarks had been reported to correct the record.

Some have argued that the World Bank did not do enough to embrace all points of view, including opponents of the project. This is a misreading of what actually happened. The communications strategy actively mined the communications of project opponents to see where the project might be vulnerable or weak, and what steps could be taken to improve the project. In fact, the communications team was encouraged to make sure the views of such critics were represented in internal discussions, putting forward awkward issues and challenging viewpoints. The World Bank also responded to NGO questions publicly, posting replies on the Bank's NT2 Web site so that unfiltered information was disseminated more widely. At other times, the Bank explained its position in opinion articles in newspapers.

The World Bank was also keen to hear directly from NGOs instead of simply responding to them. When one NGO sent a letter to the Bank's Board of Executive Directors warning that NT2 would "generate wildlife carnage on a scale never before seen in Southeast Asia," the Bank wrote back and asked for the basis for this important, if startling, conclusion. Had the World Bank issued a report containing such language, it would have quite rightly been expected to have a firm, factual basis. There was, of course, no such report and no basis for making such remarks. The hyperbole was designed to attract attention and further polarize debate. The Bank team ensured that the people who had seen the inflammatory letter also saw the subsequent letter from the NGO that contained the telling admission that the Bank could "choose to call it carnage or not."

The Context for Communications: The Legacy of Failed Hydro Projects

NT2 followed a number of hydro projects that had failed, been withdrawn, or become entangled in controversy. These projects left the World Bank bruised and confused, with some staff eager to do things better and other staff worried that hydro was too risky and time consuming. The unfortunate trail of projects had also created a presumption of guilt in the minds of many Bank-watchers: if these earlier projects had turned out poorly, surely NT2 would be the same.

In the end, this history worked in the World Bank's favor. Staff working on the project were aware of the risks and receptive to communications support that could make things easier. The past also contained valuable lessons—about the risks of staff being distracted from their functions, about allowing the Bank's efforts to be defined by others, and about failing to ensure that the Bank was open to hearing views, however disagreeable, and willing at all times to be frank about the project and its difficulties.

Heeding these lessons helped the World Bank focus on the real challenges of a complex project as reasons for the World Bank Group to be involved, not as problems that should scare off the Bank or that the Bank created. Illegal logging, for example, was a reality in part of the project area. The Bank discussed it as a reality, and was open in disclosing what it knew (and in explaining that there were things it didn't know). The Bank explained in print that NT2 was not a perfect project, but that perfect projects did not exist. Telling the truth, admitting mistakes, and discussing possible shortcomings changed the whole debate, from one in which the World Bank was defending the project to one in which the Bank was explaining the project. This shift also reinforced the third pillar of the framework, under which support would be given or withheld. The government was actively winning support from the international community *at the same time as it was signaling* that it was taking responsibility for the project. This was important, especially given the lack of first-hand knowledge of Lao PDR beyond its immediate regional neighbors.

The Media Strategy

The presence of empowered and qualified World Bank communications staff in the field proved valuable. They were able to cultivate media contacts; engage them on the various issues surrounding NT2; and grant access to project developers, government officials, and World Bank staff. Having staff in the field helped the Bank model transparency. The Bank's media team was straightforward in dealings with the press; acknowledged where there were problems and what was being done to address them; and worked to establish strong relationships of trust before the project began attracting attention. These efforts paid significant dividends. Having an effective team in place in-country also helped the World Bank be aware of local news stories and respond to NGO allegations (pitched to the local media by NGOs).

Stakeholder Engagement and Disclosure

The government, which did not have a reputation for openness, embraced the idea of releasing information and discussing the proposed project. It surprised many people by embarking on a series of consultations in Bangkok, Tokyo, Paris, and Washington, DC. Government officials also worked with a consultant to release information and respond to interviews. Their commitment to openness went beyond the project and was soon reflected in newsletters and opinion articles emerging from Vientiane.

Having the government actively advocating its case made it easier for the World Bank and other external partners to play their proper roles. Instead of being the defender of a "Bank project," the World Bank and other partners were able to explain the basis of their support for a Lao government project.

The government's commitment to the communications plan, based on a genuine commitment to transparency backed up by actions, was a turning point for NT2. A real partnership was forged between government, project developers, the World Bank, and other development partners to carry out a number of wide-ranging transparency initiatives. These coordinated, intensive efforts included promoting transparency and information disclosure throughout the project cycle, engaging in dialogue with a broad range of stakeholders, forcefully countering misinformation, providing useful context where needed, and remaining consistent with the message that the project was worth considering because of the benefits it could bring to poverty reduction and environmental protection efforts in Lao PDR.

One of the most important aspects of the strategy was to build the capacity of the government to undertake communications and consultations, not just for the NT2 project but also for all future development projects. The government's strategy focused on building the case for why this project was needed in simple terms; explaining due diligence regarding safeguards; ensuring that the consultations process was meaningful, balanced, and transparent; increasing responsiveness to NGOs and the media; making a real commitment to disclosing information; and maintaining messages consistent with those of the the developers, the World Bank and other partners. The government made good use of technical assistance in the form of communications and consultations expertise, based in government offices in Vientiane.

Finally, the World Bank's communications effort did not stop work once the project was approved by the Board of Executive Directors. Management recognized that the success of the project would depend on implementation of all parts of the agreement—from those touching on the engineering and economic aspects to those affecting its environmental and social aspects. The Bank's commitment to being unafraid to be responsive to news—both favorable and unfavorable—and finding areas for improvement was sincere. It wanted this process to continue through implementation, so that it could help ensure that the project delivered on its promise to the people of Lao PDR. The Bank's communications group continued to work closely on NT2 as a priority, placing a member in Vientiane to work directly with groups visiting the site, keeping a blog on project visits, and answering questions on the spot.

Why the World Bank's Communication Strategy Worked

Several factors worked in the World Bank's favor; none was more important than that the wider project team focused intently on getting all operational details right. There was no tolerance for cutting corners, no hiding of difficult issues. This was a project that likely could stand up to scrutiny. The Bank team working on NT2 included a number of seasoned communications professionals with experience in difficult projects. This experience translated into both practical knowledge (of the value of speed and transparency, for example) and credibility in discussions with non-communications colleagues in the Bank. The communications specialists also knew the region well, having worked in East Asia for between four and eight years, and having spent time in Lao PDR, some on many occasions. The wider communications team—which was scattered across Asia, Europe, and the United States and met via teleconference, sometimes on a weekly basis—had specific knowledge of local audiences, different constituencies, and the World Bank itself. Most knew each other and had worked together. They shared information and ideas openly, cooperated well, and fully recognized that NT2 was a priority, given the World Bank's checkered record of infrastructure projects in the 1990s.

The Bank managed to create a system of clearance that allowed it to respond to any question or news article in the same news cycle. This was no small feat in a large organization spanning all time zones, with headquarters 12 hours behind the Asian offices. That this was achieved attests to the trust of senior management (field-based management were always involved and consulted), which allowed communications staff to give live interviews, write letters to the editor, and answer questions from the media and civil society without having to wait for overnight approval, as is often required in high-profile projects.

Conclusion

NT2 needs to be seen in the context of the projects that came before it and the lessons learned from them. These lessons encouraged World Bank management to have a strong communications presence in the team evaluating the project, with a mandate to provide an open flow of information and to ensure that the Bank defined its own position all along. The high technical standards of the project provided a solid basis for a communications strategy based on transparency, and the communications strategy, in turn, helped inform the project team of risks and external views. The Bank stuck to these simple rules and sought to hold its critics to the same standard of accuracy and openness. The Bank benefited greatly from advice from many sources, especially from well-informed Lao experts who were neutral toward NT2. The Bank team worked well together and maintained openness and cohesion throughout many months, even years, extending beyond Board approval.

Can This Approach Be Replicated in Other Hydro Projects?

Project staff in the World Bank and elsewhere have looked at NT2, and many have drawn the wrong conclusion. Some have argued that because the project took so many years to come to fruition, the costs and delays make such projects financially unviable. Others have concluded that the extensive support given to NT2 from senior management and senior communications staff cannot be replicated without bringing other Bank business to a halt. Both conclusions are flawed. NT2 was not just a major project; it was the largest and most controversial project the World Bank took on after a wave of projects that had caused serious internal problems and doubt. NT2, like it or not, had to deal with legacy issues. Thanks to the success of NT2, hydro projects today do not carry the same burden. Provided the same commitment is there to openness, transparency, and pro-activity, as well as the mandatory high standards of operational accuracy, there is no reason why other projects should not succeed.

NT2 shows that a properly structured and executed communications component can pay large dividends. It can improve project quality, by bringing in critical information that might otherwise be ignored or viewed defensively. And it can create a space for technical experts to do what they are trained to do instead of being distracted by well-orchestrated media campaigns by groups with no goal but to stop a project from proceeding. The biggest lesson is not that NT2 received special communications support but that too many important projects run needless risks of disruption and failure by underinvesting in communications.

Images from the Nam Theun 2 Project

The Nam Theun River is harnessed to provide power and generate income that will help the Lao people

The natural environment and traditions are being respected

The lives of those living on the Nakai Plateau are changing

Improving the People's Lives

Better housing provides lasting benefits

New houses were designed and located in consultation with villagers . . .

. . . and are far better than the older houses

Improving the People's Lives

Villagers enjoy clean water supply near to their houses

New village infrastructure is appreciated by villagers

Having electricity raises living standards

Improving the People's Lives

Village children
have new schools . . .

. . . and villagers enjoy
better health services

Improving the People's Lives

Reservoir fishing provides food and income

Agriculture remains a central livelihood activity, and irrigation expands opportunities

Rice remains important

Improving the People's Lives

A variety of livelihood activities are encouraged

Mushrooms are grown for consumption and sale

Some villagers have opened small restaurants

Others have opened small shops

Traditional activities like weaving continue to be important as well

Improving the People's Lives

Village forestry
activities augment
resettlers' incomes

Some villagers raise
fish in ponds

Buffalo remain an important
asset for families

Pictorials are used during
discussions with villagers to
illustrate livelihood concepts

Protecting the Natural Environment

NT2 supports
conservation
of the vast NT2
Watershed, an area
of global biodiversity
significance

In the Watershed,
development and
conservation are
delicately balanced

Efforts are made to
improve lives while
promoting sustainability
of the natural resources

Protecting the Natural Environment

Preserving cultural heritage is important

Temple structure

Traditions have to be respected as new ways are introduced

Protecting the Natural Environment

Fauna and flora have to be protected . . .

. . . as do the
various habitats

Protecting the Natural Environment

Close monitoring addressed environmental impacts from construction

Re-vegetation was done to restore disturbed areas, such as this embankment near the Intake Structure

Impacts are being monitored closely, such as on the Xe Bang Fai River, which receives water downstream of the powerhouse

A robust water quality monitoring effort is ongoing

Building the Physical Project

The Nakai Dam
under construction

Construction of the
Regulating Dam, which helps
manage downstream releases
of water used for generation

The Nakai Dam
during gate testing

Building the Physical Project

Powerhouse area as it looked during the early construction phase

Turbine assembly and installation

NT2 Power house, where generation occurs

Building the Physical Project

Switchyard,
where electricity
transitions from the
powerhouse to the
transmission system

Transmission lines, which
evacuate power from the
generation station and
bring it to the users

Construction included excavating several tunnels and access adits

Building the Physical Project

Road and bridge improvements were also part of the project

New Thalang Bridge, with old bridge visible behind it

The 27-km-long Downstream Channel carries water from the Regulating Dam to the Xe Bang Fai River

The Downstream Channel passes through a tunnel, which was constructed by the project

Building the Physical Project

Pedestrian and tractor crossings provide safe access for villagers working in the fields to both sides of the channel

An aeration weir structure in the channel improves water quality (water becomes more oxygenated as it flows over the weir)

Independent monitoring remains critical to preserving the gains achieved

CHAPTER 6

Some Cross-Cutting Lessons

Duke Center for International Development

Preparation of the Nam Theun 2 (NT2) project represented a milestone in World Bank history. It tested the World Bank's ability to engage in a challenging large-scale hydropower project in a poor country in a way that promotes economic growth, spurs social development, and reduces poverty; avoids the natural resource curse; and applies sound environmental and social safeguards. An unusually committed, dedicated, and persistent staff faced many challenges that could not have been predicted at the outset. Although many participants and stakeholders criticized the long and costly preparation of NT2, to a large extent its ultimate approval by the Board reflected the careful and comprehensive process by which it was prepared and appraised.

Criticisms of the World Bank may partly reflect participants' failure to fully understand the roles and expectations of all stakeholders. Developers may have expected the World Bank to act as a deal maker, whereas senior Bank management saw the Bank's role as that of a gatekeeper focused on issues that would be deal breakers for its Board. Many of the critical incidents that occurred during project preparation have been caused by the fact that all

The chapter, produced by the Duke Center for International Development (DCID), provides an external look at the World Bank's preparation of the NT2 project. It is based on the review and analysis of project documentation, a one-day workshop with selected NT2 team members, and various meetings and discussions with stakeholders. The team that prepared the report was led by the late Dennis Rondinelli and Gary Nelson (University of North Carolina) and included Jonathan Abels, Rosemary Fernholz, Francis Lethem, and Natalia Mirovitskaya.

participants at times overlooked or ignored issues that were considered potential deal breakers for other participants.

At the same time, the growing belief among World Bank staff that key officials in the government shared their objective of using NT2 to improve the lives of the poor in Lao PDR allowed the World Bank and the government to become more flexible. They began with agreement on the desired result of "doing the project right" and worked backward through the technical steps and processes that would be needed to arrive at that end. During every critical incident, strategically positioned World Bank staff stepped up and demonstrated leadership to make sure that the process stayed on track and the end goal was kept in mind.

NT2 was riddled with tensions between the World Bank's insistence on compliance with all 10 of its safeguards and the highest-quality technical preparation on the one hand and the developers' perception that the Bank was adding costly analyses and slowing progress toward approval on the other. The tensions may have arisen because the developers and the World Bank did not reach full agreement up front on the scope of safeguard work required for such a complex project. Investors need to be committed to addressing environmental and social issues as an integral part of project design and cost estimation. The experience of NT2 has shown that this can be achieved if the two parties agree on the key actions required for a safeguards work program.

Clear understanding of the project's challenges and critical incidents is necessary if the lessons of experience learned during NT2 are to be applied in the preparation of similar projects in the future. World Bank staff and managers need greater awareness of the issues that can become deal breakers before embarking on megaprojects in poor countries.

An essential lesson of NT2 is that in a project with multiple participants, developers, and stakeholders, each group has a set of objectives and criteria that are not always consistent with those of other participants. Understanding what constitutes acceptable criteria for participation and what may constitute a potential deal breaker is crucial for planning project preparation and implementation and in developing an acceptable financial arrangement.

The process of project preparation—in which the World Bank participated for nearly a decade—offers a rich set of lessons for Bank staff and other stakeholders on how complex infrastructure projects financed through public-private partnerships in poor countries can be prepared and appraised more effectively. The lessons of NT2 that distinguish it from previous World Bank hydropower projects can be categorized into six areas. These lessons reflect what NT2 project preparation team members and internal stakeholders believe the World Bank did effectively and successfully, as well as aspects of the project's preparation that could have been improved.

It is emphasized that the role of the World Bank was strongly shaped by two factors: (i) timing of NT2 as the World Bank reengaged in hydropower projects and as World Bank safeguards were evolving; and (ii) the specific circumstances of the project itself, in particular the magnitude and risk of the project and the development stage of the country. In general, the role of the World Bank in a project is sized to the scale and complexity of the project. In the case of NT2, there was broad scope and need for a very high level of engagement. The role of the World Bank, as discussed below, must be considered in this light.

1. Strengthen Government Capacity

The World Bank's participation in project preparation shifted perceptions of NT2. Without World Bank participation, the project likely would have focused narrowly on the energy component: a large-scale dam and hydropower project using Lao resources. With World Bank participation, the project scope broadened to become a significant investment for stimulating economic growth, spurring social development, providing more reliable energy sources, reducing poverty, and strengthening the government's financial management and governance capacity.

To achieve these objectives, the World Bank focused on applying safeguards that sought to ensure that NT2's construction and operation would not adversely affect the Lao people and that the government developed sufficient financial management and administrative capacity to prepare the project for appraisal, allocate revenues for development purposes, and use project revenues to improve the lives of the poor. Strengthening the capacity of the government and promoting policy reform were preconditions for the World Bank's approval of NT2 as a social development and poverty reduction project. Doing so represented a continuing challenge throughout project preparation.

The World Bank's willingness to participate in the project was based on the government's commitment to use revenues from the sale of hydropower to reduce poverty and provide effective environmental and social protection. To address the serious weaknesses in the government's budget preparation, execution, and control systems, the World Bank sought improvements in its expenditure management, including fiscal planning and budget preparation, treasury, and accounting and reporting; development of information systems; and adoption of a legislative framework for public expenditure management.

Over time, the World Bank placed increasing financial management requirements on the government, despite the government's insistence on minimal intrusions in its internal affairs. The Bank's NT2 team had to find a balance between what would satisfy the World Bank's Board and what would be acceptable to the government.

Salient Positive Features of NT2

The World Bank used several approaches to meet the challenges of transforming NT2 into a development and poverty reduction project. To overcome potentially adverse uses of revenues from the project, it embedded NT2 in a broader development strategy that specifically addressed the objective of reducing poverty and promoting development. Over time, the World Bank worked with the government to strengthen its institutions and processes by making them more transparent and accountable

The salience of governance issues also increased because of the stronger recognition that governance issues were crucial to the disposition of revenues. World Bank staff responded by engaging in more intense dialogue with the government on the use of the revenues from the project in ways that would contribute to poverty alleviation. The Bank's discussions led to agreements on the management of finances, transparency in the budgeting and expenditure processes, and the importance of investments in social services.

The World Bank determined that the government was seriously committed to poverty reduction and economic reform based on the country's record of social improvements, poverty reduction, and structural adjustment. It was essential to the World Bank that the NT2 project be prepared within a decision framework with specific performance objectives that the government had to meet before the World Bank would formally present the project to its Board for approval.

In preparing NT2, World Bank staff learned how important it is to identify critical capacity weaknesses early in the project cycle and to follow up quickly in designing and reaching agreement with the government on a capacity-building strategy for which it will take ownership. Experience with NT2 illustrated that to be effective, the capacity-development strategy needs to be embedded in, and built on, country systems and processes, making government processes and policies more open and transparent, more sharply focused on poverty, and more oriented toward achieving results.

Because public finance management reforms were slow and the World Bank's senior management had strong doubts that the system could be strengthened within five years, the Bank approved a two-track approach to improving the government's public finance management. Track One used a sequence of Poverty Reduction Support Credits/Operations to support and monitor progress on this program; an ongoing Financial Management Capacity Building Credit financed technical assistance.

Track Two established specific revenue-management arrangements for NT2 revenues. These arrangements were designed to monitor the flow of NT2 revenues and expenditures even if the overall system was not yet strong enough to do so. Frequent and numerous informal discussions between the NT2 team and regional managers convinced senior World Bank officials that the two-track approach was both effective for achieving results and acceptable to the government and other stakeholders. These meetings and the arguments presented by midlevel management and its public financial management team played a critical role in convincing World Bank senior management of the viability of this approach.

Areas for Improvement

The World Bank assigned a competent and dedicated team to NT2 and worked flexibly within its procedures to support a social development and poverty reduction strategy. Experience gained during project preparation suggests some improvements that may make the process more effective if such a strategy is used in similar projects in the future:

- Develop basic measurements for the skills required in complex project finance transactions, in order to estimate the level of capacity at the start of preparation, during preparation, and at financial close. Early in the project cycle, identify the means of addressing core capacity deficits (study tours, comprehensive project finance training, concession-management training, and other mechanisms).
- Create a power-influence-capability mapping of key stakeholders and identify modes of engagement that could simultaneously build trust with and competence within counterpart organizations. Staff came to recog-

nize that the World Bank must accept the fact that some project conditionalities may be unpalatable to the client. Additional efforts may be needed to explain the rationale and to help clients develop the technical skills to meet these requirements. Similarly, it became evident that in some cases the clients may be reluctant to borrow additional money to build capacity as long as the World Bank remains formally uncommitted to the project and may withdraw at any time. Through dialogue and constructive exchange of ideas, mutually acceptable modalities (such as tapping related already-funded efforts to cover necessary ground) can be found to accomplish the desired objectives.

- Identify broad priority programs (such as primary education and primary health), and develop agreements with the government on reforms needed to ensure that funds targeted to these areas can be efficiently and transparently applied for their intended purposes. Identifying priority programs would allow a functional or even administrative classification of expenditures, making it easier for the World Bank and the government to agree on necessary improvements to be undertaken in the context of the Poverty Reduction Strategy Paper and planning and budgeting cycles.

- Early on, encourage the government to strengthen its capacity to use project revenues effectively for social development and poverty reduction. In future projects, the World Bank should focus on training government officials in budgeting, treasury management, accounting, and reporting as well as on developing basic systems and regulations. It should also expose senior government officials to experiences in countries with effective financial management practices.

2. Build Trust between the World Bank and the Client

Throughout the preparation of NT2, especially in the early stages, the World Bank faced the challenge of creating sufficient trust between the government and the Bank's senior managers and staff. The government and the developers were initially reluctant to involve the World Bank, because of fears that its conditionality would impinge on the sovereignty of the government and create additional delays. The World Bank's senior management was uncertain about the government's financial management capacity and its commitment to using revenues from NT2 for poverty reduction and environmental management.

To bridge the gap between the two perspectives—and to find and strengthen the common ground (that is, agreement on the importance of achieving the development objectives embodied in NT2)—the World Bank used a negotiating and communications instrument (the decision framework), which was agreed with the government during a management mission led by the country director in August 2001. The decision framework established clear signals that project preparation would be linked to the government's progress in implementing plans and policies for reducing poverty and protecting the environment; taking action that would reduce technical, financial, and economic risks; applying safeguard policies that met World Bank standards; and obtaining support from international donors and civil society for implementation of the project.

Salient Positive Features of NT2

Building trust with the government required extensive knowledge of the country's political and cultural conditions and the formal and informal rules through which decisions were being made. The World Bank was gradually able to develop trust because the team assigned to the project worked persistently to understand and become more sensitive to the political and cultural situation in Lao PDR. This process was aided by the growing collaboration between the World Bank and the Asian Development Bank (ADB), which had deeper regional ties and relationships with Lao PDR. World Bank staff noted the importance of openness, respect, and consistency in dealing with government officials in order to build the required level of trust. Frank explanations of the challenges facing the successful appraisal of the project were spelled out clearly by the project oversight group in 2003.

A strong and continuing field presence was also crucial in developing trust and, more broadly, facilitating project preparation. The continuing field presence was especially important in light of the weaknesses in government capacity and the amount of follow-up needed by the World Bank team. Close and continued contact with the government maintained and deepened the level of trust during project preparation.

The trust between the World Bank and the government grew throughout project preparation, especially between 2002 and 2005, as the government provided both symbolic and substantive signs of commitment to make the project an effective instrument of poverty reduction. The World Bank also helped gradually build trust and credibility among its staff, the government, and the developers by setting milestones and allowing sufficient time for participants to meet them. Given the long project preparation process, the quality of stakeholder engagement the NT2 team was able to achieve proved critical in maintaining commitment to the project.

Areas for Improvement

The World Bank could improve its interactions with the government and other partners and build trust more quickly by clearly assessing—early on—fundamental objectives and operational constraints of the client and partners, organizational arrangements, and the most pressing capacity constraints. Discussions also suggest that the Bank needs to be clear about which requirements and standards are nonnegotiable and proactively communicate the reasons why it is in the best interest of the country's development to comply with them. It could do so by drawing on the World Bank's relevant experience elsewhere and developing a shared understanding of risks and rewards with the government.

3. Apply Sound Environmental and Social Safeguards

The World Bank's participation in the NT2 project raised important challenges in ensuring that environmental and social safeguards were applied in the four major impact areas: the Nakai plateau, where most of the resettlement would take place; the NT2 watershed; the downstream area along the Xe Bang Fai (XBF) River and its tributaries; and the downstream area along the lower Nam Theun River and its tributaries. Preparation of the NT2 project was unusual, because it required application of all 10 of the World Bank's safeguards. The World Bank worked closely with the government and other partners to ensure that project appraisal, design, and implementation programs adequately addressed potential environmental and social impacts and risks.

Because under the policy of the World Bank many of the people in the region affected by the project are considered to be Indigenous Peoples (ethnic minorities), the Bank required preparation of a Social Development Plan with a special section on ethnic minorities. Despite the government's concern about the extent to which communities would receive special treatment based on ethnicity, the World Bank also insisted on "meaningful" community consultations that specifically addressed ethnic minority needs.

The World Bank faced several challenges in applying environmental and social safeguards, which it addressed through the Environmental Assessment and Management Plan (EAMP), the Social Development Plan (SDP), and the Social and Environment Management Framework and First Operational Plan (SEMFOP). The government, the Nam Theun 2 Power Company (NTPC), and other stakeholders thought that the World Bank was continuously expanding both the geographical scope and the thematic coverage of the analysis. NTPC claimed that by increasing demands for economic and social analysis the World Bank was "shifting goalposts" without clearly defining an acceptable set of requirements. Tensions arose because other stakeholders (including NGOs as well as some of the international financial institutions) believed that the environmental and social analyses were not comprehensive and that some essential potential problems or groups of people who would be affected by the project were ignored.

Salient Positive Features of NT2

Experience with applying the World Bank's safeguards in the NT2 project yielded several important lessons. The World Bank played an important role in supporting the development of the terms of reference for essential social studies to be undertaken by the developer. Together with two international NGOs (the International Union for Conservation of Nature [IUCN] and CARE), the World Bank supported local consultations with communities affected by the project. Although the developers criticized the number and frequency of studies as being too stringent, too time-consuming, and too costly, the application of the safeguards reduced the project's overall risk and increased credibility with a wide range of stakeholders.

The World Bank's participation in NT2 led to creation of an Environmental and Social Panel of Experts that was instrumental in advocating, designing, and monitoring the implementation of environmental and social safeguards. Formation of an independent Panel was proposed early in the project preparation process but was not implemented until 1997, after the World Bank became a more active participant in the project.

Implementing the safeguards in NT2 was facilitated by the fact that the World Bank's counterparts perceived them as integral to the achievement of project and development objectives. The findings from the application of the safeguards resulted in environmental and social management plans that were comprehensive in impact identification, covering the inundation area, project lands, construction camps, downstream areas, and the watershed.

The World Bank made creative use of the idea of environmental set-asides as a way to mitigate environmental impacts and ensure that the long-term environmental impacts yielded net benefits. The World Bank recognized that the area to be inundated could be "offset" by increasing the protection of adjacent areas.

The World Bank also supported the use of an innovative approach to assessing multiethnic Indigenous Peoples' needs by focusing on livelihoods and vulnerabilities. This approach provided a clear framework for designing appropriate development options. A new methodology was developed by a respected Thai community development consultant who was fluent in Laotian and had worked in Lao PDR some years earlier.

The NT2 project benefited from consultations beginning at an early stage of resettlement planning. Community feedback on preferred locations informed the resettlement strategy and the resettlement plans. The success of consultations with communities reflected in large part the fact that specialists were engaged at later stages of project preparation to improve the design of the consultation process and train facilitators.

Areas for Improvement

The World Bank should consider providing developers of proposed projects with complex environmental and social impacts with a framework that outlines its requirements and procedures related to the application of its safeguard policies. Such a framework could delineate the roles and responsibilities of different parties. It could also be used to develop an explicit and integrated decision process for determining requirements for analytical studies. The project preparation framework could spell out the rationale and necessity or priority of the studies, the intended audience and dissemination approach, the decision relevance and time frame, and quality standards and expectations.

NT2 teams also suggest that early screening and scoping of environmental and social issues should be carried out using a stakeholder consultation process in order to understand the broad range of concerns and the diversity of interests and to focus project preparation on key issues. They advise the World Bank to carefully assess binding commitments—such as proposed income targets—for realism and to guard against unrealistic promises that raise expectations during the project preparation phase. At the beginning of the project cycle, the World Bank should designate one person to coordinate and oversee the safeguards work and to serve as the principal spokesperson for safeguard issues.

4. Manage Financial Risk

The World Bank faced continuing challenges during preparation of NT2 in avoiding reputational risks, anticipating the objections and complaints of critics that could have delayed the project, and mitigating risks for financing institutions and private sector partners involved in Nam Theun 2's development.[1] Seeking private capital was new and in many ways politically contentious for the government, and the political risk guarantee was a relatively novel instrument. In 1994 NT2 represented the first major cross-border hydropower sales project in Asia. Mitigating political risk and raising financing required the participation of many bilateral and multilateral agencies. Coordination among the multiple agencies depended on harmonizing policies and procedures. Significantly leveraging official financing to attract private sources of financing was another challenge. The controversial nature of the project and the intense international scrutiny meant that external risks, including reputation risks for the World Bank and other partners, had to be carefully managed.

The challenges for the World Bank have been not only to reduce risk for the organizations financing the project but also to ensure sound project preparation and design with regard to five factors:

- governance (that is, the management of revenues generated from the project)
- project economics, including Thailand's demand for power
- environmental and social impacts and the need for reliable upfront assessment, management, and monitoring throughout project implementation
- transparency and the strong interest in disclosure of the information contained in the concession agreement and the power purchase agreement
- timely and clear dialogue with the client on these issues.

The World Bank's role as the lead partner among a diverse group of private and public financial/development partners required it to ensure that project appraisal was based on strong technical work that other partners could rely on for financial due diligence, assessment of social and environmental safeguards, and designing revenue management. The viability of the public-private financing arrangement required the World Bank to take the lead on due diligence assessments related to safeguards, economic and financial analysis, procurement, revenue and expenditure management, and monitoring and evaluation. The World Bank also assisted NTPC in developing its financing package and the government in coordinating its international financial institution and bilateral equity package. (NTPC and the Electricity Generating Authority of Thailand [EGAT] negotiated the power purchase agreement without the World Bank's involvement; the financiers performed due diligence on the commercial aspects of the deal.) Although the government and NTPC negotiated the concession agreement, the World Bank provided advice when requested and helped fund legal and financial advisors to the government through credits from the International Development Association (IDA).

Salient Positive Features of NT2

From the outset, the World Bank conducted a comprehensive and integrated risk assessment of NT2. Experience with the project reveals the importance of assessing the institutional structure and capacity of the country and proponents, with emphasis on those institutions that are likely to play active roles in the project's implementation, operation, and maintenance.

The project also suggests how crucial it is for the risk analysis to focus on people living in the project area. Initial comprehensive risk analysis should include a preliminary assessment of likely environmental impacts throughout the project area and spillover effects outside the immediate impact area, environmental trade-offs that could occur as a result of the project, and the possibility of offsetting negative environmental impacts through mitigation strategies.

Despite the limited creditworthiness of Lao PDR and the large size of the project, the World Bank made a concerted effort to involve a variety of multilateral and bilateral financial institutions in the financing efforts. The resulting financing structure (matching the 50/50 dollar/baht currency split of the revenue stream, which helped mitigate currency conversion risks) would be replicable in large projects that have a revenue stream in multiple currencies. In addition to the World Bank (IDA and the Multilateral Investment Guarantee Agency [MIGA]), eight other official institutions ultimately provided guarantees, financing, or export credits to support NT2. Involving the other official partners as early as possible, working in close partnership with them, and having clear work-sharing arrangements were all conducive to a healthy partnership with the official agencies.

Experience with NT2 confirms that a public-private partnership financing arrangement for large complex projects requires careful handling of work-sharing arrangements and the allocation of work among the parties according to each party's comparative advantage. The World Bank played an important role in this regard. Although it performed a significant share of the due diligence work itself, particularly on social and environmental safeguards and revenue management, it reached clear agreements with partners to define areas of work responsibility.

The design of the guarantee structure and innovative ways of funding the government's equity requirements had to be tailored specifically to circumstances in the sponsoring country. This is an area in which creativity and innovation are needed. Both the World Bank and its financial partners used the long period of time taken by project preparation to hone the financial package to match the reward/risk needs of a truly diverse set of investors. This extremely complicated process was carried out without generating controversy or raising anxiety among the key stakeholders—a remarkable achievement.

Areas for Improvement

Criticism regarding the government's poor governance record and the notion that affected persons might not feel free to openly voice their concerns in the Lao political and cultural context did not figure prominently in the first phase of World Bank involvement, from 1994 through 1997. It was not until the second period of involvement, after international civil society organizations voiced their concerns, that the World Bank took these criticisms more seriously.

Discussions on lessons learned suggest that the institution should initiate a dialogue with government early in project preparation on issues of corruption, equitable treatment of those affected by the project, transparent and accountable use of revenues, and provision of social services. Although these are difficult issues in many countries, the penalties for not raising them at an early stage can be heavy; failing to address these issues can increase uncertainties for the developers and cause costly delays in moving the project toward approval and construction.

In large infrastructure projects with high visibility, there is an inherent strain between letting the developers and the borrower know as early as possible the conditions under which the World Bank will participate in the project and risking the Bank's reputation by making that determination without having completed due diligence and assessed the impacts on all stakeholders. This was a continuing dilemma for World Bank management, given that the ultimate decisions on project approval are taken by the World Bank's Board and not its management. Nevertheless, the World Bank may have been too cautious in not sharing its thinking with the government and the developers earlier and leaving the decision on its eventual participation open for too long. Given the experience of NT2—which has increased stakeholders' awareness of the risks involved in large, complex projects, the costs associated with delays, and the World Bank's caution—the Bank should be able to signal its intentions on ultimate involvement earlier in the future.

World Bank senior management and staff need to better understand the conditions and constraints of private investors in large infrastructure projects and to make clear to potential investors early in the project cycle the Bank's limitations in meeting investors' expectations. The World Bank's institutional tendency toward risk aversion in high-visibility projects may need to be moderated by encouraging staff to discuss appropriate risk-management strategies during the review process. In large infrastructure projects with high visibility, it is important for the World Bank to encourage detailed risk identification early in the project preparation cycle and to develop more realistic risk-mitigation measures rather than to attempt to cover all risks. Trying to be too comprehensive can lead to risk-avoidance strategies rather than appropriate risk management. If it decides to pursue project preparation, the World Bank should follow up quickly with a decision framework along the lines of that adopted in NT2.

The World Bank needs to be more sensitive to cost considerations and to ensure early on in the preparation process that the financial and other costs that developers need to bear be clearly identified and agreed to by all parties. A more nuanced risk-management approach would identify and deal with key risks early in the process and leave other, less crucial issues to be dealt with later, as more facts emerge during detailed project preparation.

Processing efficiency could be improved by involving a smaller number of participants (each taking up a larger share of the financing). In future projects, the World Bank should decide early in the preparation cycle how many official agencies and commercial banks need to be involved. It should then involve them earlier on in the process and allow them to participate fully in decisions about risk mitigation.

5. Engage and Communicate with Stakeholders, Partners, and the Public

The World Bank faced the critical challenge of designing and implementing an effective consultation process that engaged all stakeholders and participants—no easy task given the controversial nature of all large hydropower projects and the low levels of trust among stakeholders that characterized the early stages of NT2. As early as 1991, when the idea of a dam on the Nam

Theun was first discussed, it generated criticism from NGOs and international civil society. When the World Bank began to participate in the project, in 1994, it was clear that it would have to develop a strategy for establishing credibility with mainstream NGOs.

The willingness of the government to participate in a consultation and public information process on NT2 was a milestone that indicated its commitment to environmental and social safeguards and to transparency. World Bank staff considered the consultation process remarkably open and wide ranging in the Lao context. Although some stakeholders criticized the way in which this process was carried out, it demonstrated the government's willingness to go beyond its normal limits in informing the public of the consequences of a major infrastructure project.

In addition to public communications, the World Bank also set up an internal communication system to meet the needs of staff working on different aspects of the project appraisal and to respond to issues of concern to members of the Bank's Board. World Bank staff created a matrix that identified the issues raised by each Board member and a record of responses and actions taken on each issue. The World Bank also provided information on NT2 to key government leaders, including legislators, NGOs, and the media. The World Bank trained key project staff members on effective communications and coordinated visits, telephone conversations, media interviews, and opinion and editorial pieces for major international and regional media.

Salient Positive Features of NT2

World Bank staff discovered that effective communication with stakeholders can both improve project design and implementation and reduce the inevitable criticism of large-scale infrastructure projects. Criticism in the international press by NGOs led to more clarity in World Bank staff's thinking about environmental and social consequences. Information disclosure and consultation were crucial to ensure the effectiveness and sustainability of NT2, inform debate, enhance transparency and accountability, strengthen public support, reduce risks, facilitate collaboration among stakeholders, and improve the quality of project design and implementation.

Experience with NT2 reveals the importance of early engagement with key partners and stakeholders in gaining agreement and buy-in of multiple parties. In addressing this challenge, the World Bank drew on, and expanded, the experience of other large infrastructure projects—for example, the Chad-

Cameroon pipeline and the Bujagali Hydropower Project in Uganda—in designing its engagement and communications strategy.

An important feature of communication in NT2 was dissemination of information in both English and local languages. The experience with NT2 also illustrates that development and implementation of local consultations can build a cadre of local facilitators and ensure that they are trained and empowered to serve as an ongoing and credible resource to the community. NT2 team reports point out that the effectiveness of the communications and consultation processes with the people affected by the project depended on the training and use of village facilitators selected from the villages to conduct consultations. The village facilitators worked closely with district officials, who were largely observers and advisors.

Finally, experience with NT2 suggests the importance of viewing communications and consultations as ongoing processes, especially in a project involving widespread resettlement in which people are expected to adopt new livelihoods. Local consultations continue in support of livelihood development, as well as with respect to downstream program implementation efforts. Communications efforts, such as the NT2 Web sites of the developer and the World Bank, as well as the government's Web site (which goes beyond NT2 to provide information on the energy sector), are also continuing, as are periodic stakeholder discussions.

Areas for Improvement

Although the international workshops held for NT2 were valuable and represented an extraordinary display of openness by the government of Lao PDR, they demanded significant resources, and in particular, time during preparation. Some World Bank staff concluded that it may not be necessary to make international workshops a modus operandi for all infrastructure projects; such workshops may be needed only in highly controversial projects in which there is strong international concern from a diversity of stakeholders including governments, civil society organizations, and/or nongovernmental organizations. If the World Bank supports future international workshops, it should continue to use independent moderators; maintain open doors to supporters, opponents, and those who are undecided; and actively recruit attendance and representation of diverse viewpoints—all of which it did in NT2. The Bank should provide background materials well in advance and in forms that are easily accessible and comprehensible to the public.

6. Maintain Oversight and Management in Complex Infrastructure Projects

A continuing challenge for the World Bank during preparation of NT2 was maintaining cohesion and oversight in project management. Effective coordination mechanisms were needed to do so. World Bank senior management believed that the elaborate structure of oversight and monitoring groups was necessary in NT2 because of the project's high visibility and the potential criticism from international civil society organizations. The independent expert panels, particularly the International Advisory Group and the Environmental and Social Panel of Experts, were essential for providing credibility to project preparation through an independent and reliable review process. The intensive oversight provided by regional management was critical to ensure a unified approach to controversial issues, some of which carried serious reputational risks for the World Bank.

Salient Positive Features of NT2

Many of the World Bank's NT2 staff felt that the project was developed in an organic fashion, fully integrated with the development framework for Lao PDR; they believed that this approach was crucial to the project's effectiveness. They emphasize that in complex hydropower and other infrastructure activities the World Bank should avoid "projectizing" the various components in ways that undermine attention to cross-cutting issues and integrated oversight.

A key to maintaining oversight and to demonstrating institutional commitment to a large and complex infrastructure project such as NT2 was establishing an institutional "home" for NT2 in the World Bank. The formation of the project oversight group at Bank headquarters had a dramatic impact on the extent to which the NT2 project proceeded in an integrated and coordinated manner. The ongoing participation and oversight of the International Advisory Group served to "keep the World Bank honest" in terms of ensuring that preparation efforts (and implementation supervision) contributed to achievement of the project's development objectives.

The individuals involved in preparing NT2 and the Poverty Reduction Support Credits had an unusual combination of strong technical skills, keen political and cultural awareness of the country, strong understanding of the workings of World Bank bureaucracy, and an outstanding client orientation.

These skills are critical in preparing a project like NT2. Interviews with management and staff alike reveal a strong shared commitment to the development of the country.

The World Bank's decision to create two separate but related projects—the NT2 project itself (supported by the guarantee operation) and the Nam Theun 2 Social and Environment Project (a grant operation covering certain NT2 environmental and social activities that were obligations of the government, and counting as part of the government's equity in the project), each with its own task team leader—enabled operational details to be more tailored and responsive to objectives. The two projects had a single project appraisal document, which simplified documentation and provided an integrated account of both aspects of NT2.

Areas for Improvement

Because of NT2's complexity, the long period of preparation, continuing uncertainties, and unanticipated events in appraising the project, the NT2 team and senior management had to adopt flexible and responsive operational procedures for sustaining the World Bank's involvement and dealing with emerging challenges. Discussions revealed that several organizational features of the World Bank itself, including the multisectoral nature of NT2 and the applicability of all environmental and social safeguards, made the project difficult to prepare.

World Bank senior management were intensely involved in NT2, ensuring heightened attention to reputational and other key risks and helping solidify internal consensus. At the same time, their involvement weakened the independence and authority of the team and its leader and contributed to lengthier processing times. Moreover, the elaborate oversight mechanisms (deemed necessary given the risks and profile of the project) were costly. In a high-risk, high-reward, high-visibility project, the right balance needs to be struck between continuous senior management oversight and maintenance of the team manager's authority with internal and external players.

Establishing the project oversight group helped build and manage consensus within the World Bank, and especially the Regional Management team. The amount of time and attention to detail that characterized the group's meetings made these meetings very costly, however, suggesting that such groups may be replicable only in very special circumstances in future projects.

The World Bank's decision to designate a project as a corporate priority should trigger the creation of a core team, led by a senior staff member, perhaps at the director level, that is freed from other duties for an extended period. Although this approach would not obviate the need for intensive involvement by senior management, it could curb the tendency for senior management to intervene too much by raising their comfort level and perhaps reduce the costs of project preparation.

The World Bank can exercise stronger oversight and supervision by engaging senior management early on in making critical judgments so that the team can move ahead with confidence. Discussions on lessons learned from NT2 suggest that the World Bank organize itself for complex infrastructure projects so that it can reduce transaction costs for its partners and counterparts while maintaining sound project oversight. An appropriate division of labor among project partners using the relative strengths of each can lighten the work load, reduce duplication, and increase effectiveness. Division of labor requires a relationship of mutual trust among stakeholders and a supportive bureaucracy. This is an area in which better results could have been achieved during the project development phase. Easing the work load of government counterparts is also critical, particularly given their severe capacity constraints. In this regard, good information flows and joint missions that are timed in a way that minimizes disruption to the government are particularly important.

Some NT2 team members suggest that reporting requirements that go beyond what is required by country systems should also be mutually agreed upon at the outset and should strike a balance between accountability and sufficiency. The decision framework should be linked to the overall development framework; it should serve as a guide to the decision-making process used by the team and by management.

Before supporting a megaproject, the World Bank must determine that the government has a satisfactory track record of reform and that it is committed to meeting certain development objectives. The sooner that determination can be made, the better, because clear signals early on can save time, build the confidence of other stakeholders, and enhance the likelihood of implementation success.

Note

1. The consortium known as NTEC (the Nam Theun 2 Electricity Consortium), which was formed to develop the NT2 project, was led by Electricité de France (EDF) and included the Electricity Generating Public Company Limited (EGCO) of Thailand and the Italian-Thai Development Public Company Limited (ITD). In September 2002, NTEC and the government of Lao PDR formed the Nam Theun 2 Power Company Limited (NTPC), a Lao company that would build, own, and operate the NT2 project, with the shares of NTPC owned by Electricité de France International (35 percent); the Lao Holding State Enterprise (LHSE), representing the government (25 percent); EGCO (25 percent), and ITD (15 percent). In September 2010, ITD sold its 15 percent shareholding in NTPC to EGCO (10 percent) and EDFI (5 percent).

CHAPTER 7

Reflections on Implementation

Mara T. Baranson

The story of Nam Theun 2 (NT2) implementation is a complicated and fascinating one that is still unfolding. This chapter gives a brief overview of the implementation ground covered to date, along with some preliminary reflections on what has been learned thus far.[1]

Implementing NT2

Implementation of NT2 has required the execution and coordination of thousands of interrelated tasks over a large project area, the delicate balancing of multiple goals, and the recognition of and responsiveness to the needs and preferences of a myriad of stakeholders and other interested parties. As with any large undertaking, not everything has gone as planned. The challenges have been met one way or another, however, yielding important lessons in the process. A comprehensive extraction of these lessons will have to wait until the project is completed.

During preparation, key risks to achievement of the project objectives were identified to include technical/engineering, social, and environmental risks and the risks associated with revenues, capacity, and commitment. Given the level of expertise of the project company, few doubted its ability to deliver on the technical aspects of the project. The real challenge was to ensure that the environmental and social mitigation measures undertaken kept pace with progress on construction, that the inevitably tight time frames did not compromise results, that NT2 revenues would be applied effectively and transparently to their intended productive uses, and that the capacity necessary to do the job right was developed or provided.

Meeting these challenges has required continuous effort from the start, and the challenges have been met with varying degrees of success. NT2 has been delivered broadly on time and on budget—a remarkable feat for a project of its size and complexity.

Construction of the Hydropower Facility

From the start, construction progress has been impressive: multiple civil works, spread over a large geographic footprint, have been built to international quality standards and delivered broadly on time and on budget. Key elements—including the dam, the intake structure, the powerhouse, the regulating dam, the downstream channel, and other elements—have been constructed, and the reservoir has been filled. Testing and commissioning of the elements of the hydraulic system have been completed and commercial operations have commenced. Addressing the direct environmental impacts of construction (such as dust, erosion, sediment control, and impacts on water quality) has been an ongoing challenge but one that has been met over time through persistent, close attention and through monitoring of actions and outcomes.

The handover of assets (such as project roads, which are already in the process of being transferred from the project company to the government) and programs (such as community health) has begun, and efforts to ensure that the necessary capacity building is taking place are continuing. The sustainability of the infrastructure and services will remain a challenge over the longer-term; this is not a problem of design, but rather the nature of such development efforts. Each asset or program will have slightly different time frames and risks; targeted strategies are being developed for each, tapping the potential for linkages to broader development programs under implementation in and around the NT2 area.

Financing

Financial disbursements to date on the project are in line with actual NT2 project expenditure levels and are covered by financing already arranged. The total base cost for NT2 of $1.25 billion was disbursed as of October 2009. Nam Theun 2 Power Company (NTPC) expected that the final NT2 project costs up to the commercial operations date (which occurred on April 30, 2010) would amount to $1.29 billion—an increase of $40 million over the base cost but well below the cost, including contingencies, of $1.45 billion estimated earlier. The estimates proved reliable and the additional funding has been drawn from the contingency budget, which had already been arranged.

The Legal Framework

As a large infrastructure project, NT2 was prepared, developed, and is being implemented under the terms and conditions defined in a Concession Agreement—entered into by the developer (NTPC) and the host country (Lao PDR)—and other agreements concluded respectively between the Lao PDR Government, NTPC, and other entities involved in the Project. The Concession Agreement constitutes the backbone of the Project. It is a very detailed document describing the respective rights and obligations of the Parties and applicable laws and dispute resolution mechanisms that govern their relationships. Other Agreements concluded and entered into by stakeholders directly involved in the financing, construction, and operation of the Project include: (i) the Shareholders' Agreement; (ii) the Power Purchase Agreements (PPA) between NTPC, as power supplier, and respectively, the EGAT and EDL as off-take purchasers (under these PPAs, EGAT and EDL are obliged to procure a certain amount of power produced under the Project and secure the project payment stream); and (iii) a construction contract. On the financial side, a Common Terms Agreement was entered into by the Senior Lenders and financial institutions involved in financing and guaranteeing the project. Finally, each of the respective IFIs has concluded specific Financial Agreements—covering their respective credit, grant, guarantee, and/or loan—with the Lao PDR and/or Project Agreements (PAs) with the NTPC. It must be mentioned that the Parties agreed to disclose a summary of the terms and conditions of the Concession Agreement, including all the details of the specific environmental and social provisions which form Schedule 4 to the Concession Agreement.

Macroeconomic Stability, Structural Reform, and Financial Management

Since implementation of NT2 began in mid-2005, the government has maintained relatively stable macroeconomic conditions and robust economic growth. It has adopted significant structural reforms, including in the areas of trade, business environment, private sector, and public financial management, and put new budget and audit laws in place. Through the Public Financial Management Strengthening Program (PFMSP, formerly the PEMSP), the government is establishing mechanisms to manage revenues—including those from NT2, which began to flow in 2010—with greater transparency and accountability while ensuring that they are used effectively (in the case of revenues from NT2, to support priority poverty reduction programs and improved environmental management). Work on revenue management aspects has gone well so far, although the true test will come once substantial NT2 revenues start to flow into the GOL budget system.

At this point, the public finance system strengthening is making strides toward achieving the necessary performance thresholds to render redundant the specific NT2 revenue-management arrangements, although that point will take some more years to reach. The fact that there is continued multidonor interest in supporting implementation of a sound public financial framework in Lao PDR, including related capacity-building needs, bodes well for continued progress in this area. At the same time, the specific NT2 revenue-management arrangements are at an advanced stage of preparation. Although it has taken longer than planned to reach this point, eligible programs have now been identified, and work is in progress on finalizing the implementation details. This work will be followed by the development of appropriate monitoring and reporting tools.

Capacity Building

Several thousand (over 6,000 at the peak) Lao workers received training and gained experience through working on NT2. (The inclusion of "Lao preference" requirements in legal agreements promoted using Lao workers as a large part of the labor force on the project.) This provided them with highly sought-after and marketable skills. This is substantial capacity building in a small country, because many of the skills are useful for infrastructure projects, in general—not just for hydro.

Nevertheless, capacity building under NT2 appears to have been achieved more through learning-by-doing than through planned and systematic learning and technical assistance; progress in capacity building has been more limited than it could have been. As the importance of hydropower as a least-cost, clean, renewable option grows and the number of potential projects under consideration surges, more systematic capacity building, with suitable indicators and baseline data, will be necessary to support the range of skills needed to plan, review, and undertake the types of projects that will help Lao PDR tap its enormous hydropower resources in an environmentally and socially sustainable way.

Risk Assessment

To date, most of the risks that have materialized during NT2 preparation were foreseen and have been satisfactorily addressed—some through adjustments in project design, others through comprehensive monitoring and evaluation arrangements, including joint supervision missions by international financial institutions, and guidance from the Environmental and Social Panel of Experts. A development that was not anticipated during preparation was the huge change in global energy prices in 2008—raising questions about depending on rigorous forecasts when assumptions can prove wrong. In the case of NT2, the higher prices for hydrocarbon fuels favorably affect NT2's economic viability (making alternative generation options relatively more costly).

Environmental and Social Impacts

NT2 was designed to demonstrate good practices in the environmental and social aspects with the hope that the practices would form the basis for developing national standards. An important step in the direction of developing national standards was realized with the government's promulgation of the national policy on environmental and social sustainability of the hydropower sector, in 2006.

The environmental and social impacts of NT2 play out in three main project areas. The first is the Nakai plateau, where the physical resettlement phase has been completed, with all affected villages successfully moved before the start of reservoir impoundment (mid-2008). Villagers are enjoying improved conditions, including new good-quality houses, access to clean water nearby, new schools, and improved health services. At the same time, villagers are adjusting to new livelihood options and ways of life. It will take years before villagers fully develop their livelihoods (in agriculture, village forestry, livestock, and reservoir fisheries) and develop experience with new ways of life. The resettlement period will be considered ended only when the established village and household income targets are achieved (a legal obligation of the project company, to be met within five years of relocation).

In the project lands (lands taken to make way for project structures, such as the downstream channel and transmission lines), impacts resulted primarily in the need for compensation and technical assistance on livelihood development. Although there were some delays in providing compensation (for a variety of reasons, including the need to explore alternatives to land-for-land compensation when suitable land was scarce) and a number of grievances have been raised, obstacles are being overcome, as efforts to provide technical assistance have been accelerated and grievance mechanisms improved to achieve more rapid resolution.

The second affected area is the watershed area, comprising the Nakai-Nam Theun National Protected Area and the two adjacent wildlife corridors (also protected areas), where considerable work has also taken place over the past few years. The Watershed Management and Protection Authority (WMPA), established to carry out the management plan for the watershed, is working to ensure that a sustainable balance is achieved between development and conservation objectives. Although it has experienced some teething pains, the relatively young organization is making progress in carrying out its mandate.

The third affected area is downstream of the project, including the Xe Bang Fai River downstream of the powerhouse and the Nam Theun River downstream of the Nakai Dam (up to the Theun-Hinboun headpond). A Downstream Implementation Plan, building on more than two years of investigation and pilot trials, is currently guiding implementation of programs and activities that address environmental and social impacts in these downstream areas.[2] Work on the downstream program—which consists of infrastructure provision, livelihood restoration, and fish-catch monitoring—started somewhat later than the efforts on the plateau, in part because of the timing of the impacts on the downstream areas.[3] Having overcome delays in finalizing the detailed plan, which will be operationalized as a series of rolling plans designed to offer flexibility to adapt to changing realities and to incorporate lessons as they are learned, NTPC is moving forward expeditiously. Close attention is being paid and the implementation pace is being accelerated as needed to mitigate any risks arising from the initial delays.

Keeping Stakeholders Engaged

Views about complex, high-profile projects are almost always heterogeneous. Because stakeholders have different considerations, strategies, viewpoints, and agendas, it is difficult, if not impossible, to please everyone—and doing so is not a goal. In the case of NT2, the collective goal (shared by the Government, NTPC, and the international financial institutions supporting the project) was to reach out to international stakeholders to brief them on the project and receive feedback; clearly lay out the facts, benefits, and risks; and share and exchange views on the plans to develop this complex project in a continual and dynamic way, tackling unforeseen events and developments as they arose.

Sharing information helps boost understanding, which leads to dialogue and, often, agreement and support; making available the appropriate information, in a suitable format, at the right time and frequency is also important. Having the opportunity to discuss information and exchange ideas with others is often critical to finding solutions to complex problems.

Information-sharing continues to be an important element of NT2 implementation. The momentum gained during project preparation on information-sharing with local, regional and international stakeholders has been maintained, and NTPC and the international financial institutions have done a very effective job of sharing information. The range of information made available on Web sites was commendable: an unprecedented amount of project-related information on NT2 is available to the public through the project company's NT2 Web site (http://www.namtheun2.com), the Bank's NT2 Web site (http://www.worldbank.org/laont2), and the government's NT2 Web site (http://www.poweringprogress.org), which discloses key project information along with information on the Lao power sector. However, in some respects, such as the timeliness with which information was released, improvement is needed.

Increasingly participatory local consultations continue across the various project areas, as livelihood options are tested and refined. An annual stakeholder forum (first held in 2006) provides an opportunity for a broad range of stakeholders, including local government officials, diplomats, donors, the media, and local and international civil society, to take stock of progress. Going forward, it could be a good modality for exchanging views on emerging issues relating to livelihood and regional development.

Donor roundtable meetings are routinely held as a platform for assessing progress on key initiatives receiving donor support, such as the multidonor trust fund supporting public financial management reforms and NT2 implementation. A Lao-Thai High-Level Forum, convened in 2007 by the Lao and Thai energy ministries (and supported by the World Bank), provides a modality to further the two countries' partnership on hydropower and to facilitate an exchange of views on how to enhance the quality of environmentally and socially sustainable investments in hydropower in Lao PDR.

Strong partnerships between the international financial institutions and donors have had positive ramifications for NT2 implementation, facilitating achievement of solutions to sticky issues and coordinating the involvement of a large number of interested parties participating in supervision activities, for example. Such partnerships have increased aid effectiveness, as relative strengths are tapped to provide complementary support to the government in its efforts to attain its development goals.

Monitoring Progress

Like other large and complex projects, NT2 included extensive, multilayered monitoring arrangements and frequent, detailed reporting requirements. In addition to the internal monitoring undertaken by NTPC, external monitoring, supervision, and oversight arrangements include the following:

- Two independent expert panels (an Environmental and Social Panel of Experts and a Dam Safety Review Panel), both of which report to the government
- An International Advisory Group, which reports to the World Bank
- An independent monitoring agency and the government's engineer, both of which report to the government
- An owner's engineer, who reports to NTPC
- A lenders' technical advisor, who reports to the intercreditor agent (representing the NT2 financing parties)
- Joint supervision missions by the international financial institutions.

These monitoring arrangements have added value in effectively supporting risk identification and providing guidance on identifying and implementing suitable solutions to complex issues and challenges. They have also imposed a heavy burden on NTPC, however. The need to host separate field visits from each group, usually at separate times, has interfered with the company's implementation duties. There may be room for streamlining and rationalizing the roles, responsibilities, and reporting requirements of the various groups to reduce overlaps and lower costs while retaining the effectiveness of the monitoring mechanism.

Concluding Remarks

Across the project, the necessary progress was eventually achieved, but the process was not always easy. Some key activities and programs, for example, should have—and could have—started earlier than they did.[4] At the end of the day, good results were achieved, but in some cases achieving them took extra efforts to overcome relatively late starts.

Throughout project preparation and implementation, challenges emerged that required flexibility in design and approach to define viable and sustainable solutions that would benefit the people affected by NT2. Tension between the achievement of development objectives and the completion of technical ones was constant, often stemming from differing viewpoints regarding what to emphasize when, how to manage relative risks, and how to handle changing demands given fixed resource constraints. Through relentless discussions and efforts, the responsible parties eventually achieved the necessary tandem progress for the most part. Building consensus on the back of due diligence efforts was essential to moving forward in a constructive and coordinated way.

Some preparation lessons have already informed NT2 implementation. Lessons gleaned from the years of consultations undertaken on NT2 are being applied to ongoing local consultations that are providing valuable inputs on livelihood development and implementation of the downstream program. Lessons learned from the years of stakeholder engagement and communications are guiding ongoing efforts in these areas. Experiences and lessons drawn from monitoring and supervision efforts are informing considerations of adjustments that might be made to streamline arrangements while retaining adequate coverage, thereby improving effectiveness in this area while going forward into the operation phase. There is much to be gained from a seamless transition from project preparation to implementation.

Considerable benefit can also be achieved from applying the lessons of one project to another. NT2 offers lessons—such as those pertaining to building trust and sustaining partnership, managing financial risks, and streamlining the approach and efforts needed to meet environmental and social safeguards—that can readily be applied to future efforts. Although certain aspects of NT2—including the country context, the fortuitous elements of timing and players, the availability of a nearly perfect site for hydropower—were unique, the lessons learned can surely be considered, tailored, and applied to future endeavors to impart a lasting and broad impact on sustainable hydropower development for years to come.

The NT2 experiences and practices continue to attract international interest; several countries have already expressed interest in learning from the Lao experience on NT2. The extraction and sharing of lessons—at this stage and later—will make an important ongoing contribution toward more sustainable development of hydropower resources. Only time will tell how much NT2 will have contributed to doing dams better.

Notes

1. More comprehensive and detailed treatment of NT2 implementation progress can be found in the series of joint update reports prepared by the World Bank and the Asian Development Bank and presented to their respective boards. These documents, which are made available to the public shortly after issuance, are available at the World Bank's NT2 Web site, http://www.worldbank.org/laont2 (see the "Resources" section and click on "Project Documents and Reports").
2. According to the plan, increased water flows downstream of the powerhouse along the Xe Bang Fai River will affect about 150 kilometers of river used by 67 riparian villages (and to some limited extent for fishing by many hinterland villages). Decreased water flow in the area downstream of the Nakai Dam along the Nam Theun River (up to the Theun Hinboun headpond) will affect 37 villages that make some use of the river for fishing.
3. The effects on the Nakai plateau have been felt since the closure of the diversion tunnel in April 2008. The impacts to the downstream Xe Bang Fai have been largely along the lines predicted as the project began commercial operations in late April 2010. The impacted communities are already beginning to see benefits accruing to them from the downstream program.
4. A few examples include the salvage logging operations on the plateau/reservoir area (where differences of opinion on objectives and modalities complicated agreement and plans) and the downstream program (where protracted discussions over budget and approach affected the timing of some activities).

CHAPTER 8

NT2: A Transformative Endeavor

Patchamuthu Illangovan

This chapter describes how the country is moving forward as the project goals are being realized on the ground in four areas: the development context, the hydropower facility and related infrastructure, environmental and social programs, and international support. It provides a flavor of the important challenges ahead as well as the positive changes Nam Theun 2 (NT2) has catalyzed for Lao PDR, as the project transitions to the operations phase with commissioning of the hydropower facility.

Development Context

At the time of NT2 approval, there was skepticism about whether the Lao government would deliver on its commitments to the international financial institutions and the broader international community, as its record on reforms had been mixed. By mid-2006, it was becoming increasingly obvious to many observers that the government saw NT2 as an opportunity to transform itself and improve international perceptions and confidence in its efforts by strengthening its track record; officials in important economic positions displayed strong commitment to reforms, using the project as a springboard to

The contributions to this chapter of Nanda Gasparini, Victoria Minoian, Shabih Ali Mohib, William Rex, Viengsamay Srithirath, and Renae Stenhouse, and the inputs of several others on the World Bank task team are gratefully acknowledged.

attract more foreign direct investments. Donors responded positively to this development. The World Bank and others scaled up their support (increasing their capacity on the ground) and identified development interventions to maintain the reform momentum, respecting the Lao pace. Ongoing annual budget support operations (such as the multidonor-financed Poverty Reduction Support Operations) have continued to support important reform efforts, and a number of development partners, including Australia, the European Commission, and Japan, have been integrated into the process.

With NT2 implementation well under way in 2006, elections brought in a new government, but the government's strong ownership of NT2 remained. The outgoing government presented NT2 as a singular achievement for the Lao society; the incoming administration embedded the NT2 project in its vision for a modern country that would achieve middle-income country status by 2020. Hydropower gained prominence in meeting national priorities, with a number of important political decisions made: the Ministry of Energy and Mines was created; an independent agency for Water Resources and Environment, reporting to the prime minister, was established; the status of the country's anticorruption agency (the Government Inspection Authority) was upgraded; oversight of the State Audit Organization was transferred to the legislature from the executive branch; and many new laws and decrees were enacted or upgraded to strengthen and improve governance of natural resources, ensuring greater accountability, transparency, participation, and sustainability. Not all of these reforms can be attributed directly to the NT2 project, but many were influenced by the NT2 process and led by government officials who were closely associated with the project's evolution.

NT2 is unique in the sense that it continues to remain a centerpiece of the country's political economy as well as its bilateral relations with neighboring Thailand. The two governments now have in place a power trade agreement under which Lao PDR will sell up to 7,000 MW of electricity to Thailand by 2020; Vietnam is expected to buy another 5,000 MW. Encouraged by the developments, Lao PDR has declared that it will become the "battery of South East Asia," tapping its rich water resources to address the power needs of its neighbors. This declaration has contributed to a "hydro rush" in the country, with dam builders and contractors, power utilities, and consultants descending on the country from near and far to garner shares of the market.

With nearly 70 projects on the drawing board, some important questions remain to be answered. How many of these projects are actually needed? Will they be viable and sustainable? Will they embrace the NT2 good practices?

Although developments are mostly positive, some disturbing elements are emerging amidst the flurry of activity. Of concern is the apparent departure by the Lao government from its original approach of identifying priority investments in the energy sector (through the Power Sector Development Planning process) that meet least-cost, efficiency, and sustainability criteria. Currently, private sector developers, including some that may not be reputable hydropower companies, appear to be driving the agenda. To support long-term sustainable development of the country's hydropower resources, it will be important for the government to remain focused on its priorities and core principles; to move forward in a careful and methodical way; and to return to its sound policy of following the sector strategy and plans, in which investments are prioritized, sequenced, and selected on the basis of objective criteria, including sustainability, affordability, and benefit sharing. Social responsibility must be maintained and the lessons of previous experiences used to enrich and improve future efforts.

Achievement of financial closure on NT2 in June 2005 buoyed the hydropower industry worldwide. Many countries began redrawing their energy plans to include hydropower generation, subsequently aided by the climate change debate. There was considerable interest, from many quarters, in learning more about NT2 and its evolution. Learning about NT2 and hydropower developments will continue for many years, as the industry draws vital lessons from the project's evolving practices in engineering and construction techniques, benefit sharing, environmental and social sustainability, and transparency and accountability. Through NT2, Lao PDR has a project that is playing a role in defining the direction of the industry in East Asia. The country should aim to stay that course by developing projects that are really needed and involve quality investors. It must not be forgotten that the development of NT2 took place at a time when there was heightened global scrutiny on dam building, based on widespread criticism of past projects as well as Lao PDR's standing internationally, and that project planning was perhaps more cumbersome and lengthy than needed. There are smarter and more effective ways of taking the NT2 practices and lessons forward, which include having quality investors, a sound strategy, and the needed information to ensure the project meets its energy, social, and environmental goals.

The period since NT2 approval has witnessed numerous economic reforms, partly catalyzed by NT2 but driven in particular by the political leadership's desire to achieve middle-income status for the country by 2020. This desire has provided the government with the courage to be bolder in pursuing economic reforms, which, in turn, is empowering officials to bring about the needed changes. Nevertheless, reforms, especially those in the political space, take time. There have been some noteworthy developments to date, such as the civil society decree, the media law, and the growing acceptance of more open criticism of government policies and actions by members of the National Assembly and the general public. Citizens are demanding more accountability from government; their voices will only get louder as the nexus between politics and business interests in natural resources becomes more intertwined, increasing the risk that benefits will accrue to the few rather than to all Lao people. The government is beginning to respond to some of these concerns by opening the space for civic participation. NT2 is showing the way as an example of how a natural resources project can be developed to benefit the vast majority of the people.

The NT2 implementation period coincided with the government's Seventh Five-Year National Socio-economic Development Plan (NSEDP), approved by the National Assembly in 2006. The ambitious plan outlined the building blocks for achieving the 2020 vision of becoming a middle-income country. Its pro-poor focus and participatory process were identified as strengths; the lack of robust frameworks for medium-term expenditure and for monitoring and evaluation was seen as the major gap. Improvements in the development framework yielded some positive outcomes. The growth targets were realized, with annual growth averaging nearly 7.3 percent until the onset of the global financial crisis in early 2009. (During the previous plan period, the average annual growth rate was about 5.5 percent.) By 2007, exports reached the billion dollar mark on the back of favorable commodity prices for copper and gold. Foreign direct investment edged up toward the billion dollar mark as well, and tourism arrivals reached 1.6 million visitors in 2008, twice the 2005 figure. The economy was booming, with the NT2 project contributing more than 1 percentage point to annual GDP growth through works, goods, and services.

Beyond the numbers, NT2 has been having other positive impacts on the economy. The presence of a large number of international financing parties in the NT2 deal in 2005 gave substantial name recognition to Lao PDR and its investment climate, which until then had been largely ignored by the financial community. Gradually, the investment risk perception of Lao PDR began to improve. During this time, the Lao leadership undertook road shows to several Asian capitals to promote the investment opportunities available in the country, and more regional and international investors began to knock on

Lao PDR's doors for a range of opportunities in hydropower, mining, contract farming, food processing, industrial plantations, garments, real estate, tourism, and casinos, among others. Simultaneously, long-time domestic investors began expanding their operations.

The sudden surge in investment expansion overwhelmed the country's bureaucracy at the central and provincial levels, revealing some acute weaknesses in government policies and systems. Decision making was found to be piecemeal, opaque, lengthy, and often frustrating to investors. During 2006, the government accepted the International Finance Corporation's offer to jointly host a biannual Lao Business Forum, similar to those it had been cosponsoring in Cambodia and Vietnam. The five sessions of the forum held since 2007 have provided an effective mechanism through which the private sector can engage with key government counterparts to resolve issues ranging from taxes to licenses to axle loads. The biannual sessions are preceded by deliberations of working groups. The presence of the prime minister and other government ministers at these sessions has greatly facilitated the resolution of numerous issues, particularly around investment promotion, that otherwise would have languished. The 2009 Minerals Law and the combined Investment Promotion Law emerged from dialogue that took place at the forum.

The role of NT2 in institutionalizing public-private partnership as a model of doing business deserves acknowledgment. NT2 was the third such arrangement for Lao PDR (following Theun Hinboun Power and Lang Xang Minerals) and the largest to date. NT2's contractual framework—consisting of concession, power purchase, shareholding, and financing agreements—has more or less become the norm for the government; all projects (at various stages of development) in the hydro and mining sectors now use this model, with its framework forming the basis on which project agreements, including the obligations of the developers and the state, are structured. NT2 experiences have improved Lao confidence and competence in working with foreign shareholders to better understand corporate management practices and business ethics. The Lao Holding State Enterprise, which holds the government's share in NT2, also holds the government's share in five other hydropower projects, for example; it is working with investors from China, Japan, and Thailand. Many aspects of the NT2 concession agreement are being replicated in other projects. Based on the NT2 experience, government staff are better able to analyze and assess the contractual obligations as well as risks and rewards of projects, and negotiate better terms for the country. Working with so many international financing institutions on NT2 also helped government staff better understand project financing arrangements and how attractive deals could be structured with better management of risks.

The path-breaking and wide-reaching reforms in public financial management that have been made in Lao PDR can be attributed in large part to the NT2 project. The internal debates that took place before the government agreed to the NT2 revenue management arrangements continued into the implementation stage, albeit more around how to integrate the very ambitious management arrangements into the government's public finance management system. NT2 revenue management arrangements set a high bar. The government first formulated an integrated expenditure management program, which it later enhanced to become the Public Financial Management Strengthening Program (PFMSP). The PFMSP aimed to improve the fiduciary controls in execution of expenditures (by centralizing customs, tax, and treasury functions); make budgets more policy oriented (by introducing budget norms and providing a more medium-term perspective to budgeting); bring more transparency into the use of public monies (by publishing in-year budget reports and annual financial statements); and increase the scope and coverage of external oversight over budgetary spending (by providing independence to the State Audit Office and ensuring that financial statements are audited and submitted to the National Assembly annually).

Encouraged by success, reformers gained momentum, implementing additional reforms. The new Budget Law reasserted centralized control over execution of budgets and revenue administration. This required an authorizing political environment and significant implementation capacity. Under the Consolidated Treasury Account system that was implemented, provinces relinquished direct control over their bank accounts. At the same time, the government tightened the exemption regime to ensure that tax expenditures were managed effectively. The passage and subsequent implementation of the Budget Law is a bold reform effort that spans both political and economic spheres. These efforts are beginning to pay off.

The government's commitment to reform its public finances was matched by development partners' support of a coordinated effort to implement the PFMSP. Four development partners—Australia, the European Commission, Sweden, and Switzerland—joined the World Bank to establish a multidonor trust fund to finance priority capacity development activities identified in the PFMSP Action Plan. This effort was supplemented by the World Bank's Financial Management Capacity Building Project. The Agence Française de

Développement and the Asian Development Bank also aligned their support with PFMSP priorities.

Support also came from another important source, Vietnam. Lao PDR sourced peer-to-peer learning from the Vietnamese Ministry of Finance. The World Bank facilitated access to knowledge of reform experiences from other countries, including Mongolia. The development of the Consolidated Treasury Account Framework, for example, was preceded by peer-to-peer learning (Lao-Vietnamese-Mongolian), the sharing by international experts of global practices, and work by government staff with experts to develop alternate frameworks for treasury management.

The embedding of the NT2 revenue management arrangements in the broader PFMSP has enabled work to remain largely on track since 2005. With revenues starting in mid-2010, the government identified the priority eligible programs and included them in the 2009/10 budget approved by the National Assembly in July 2009. Rural infrastructure (roads and rural electrification), education, health, and environmental protection have each received their share of the revenues. The eligible programs are consistent with the criteria set in the arrangements, including the one on additionality. The challenges going forward will be to track these expenditures, monitor performance, and audit expenses. For its part, the World Bank completed one Public Expenditure Tracking Survey and two Public Expenditure Reviews, the most recent of which reviewed the readiness of the NT2 revenue management arrangements, during the intervening years.

Without a well-developed public financial management system, the government will not be able to fully harness the benefits of its natural resources potential to improve the quality of life of its 6 million people and avoid the "resource curse" that has afflicted other resource-rich developing countries. Progress since 2005 has been impressive; if such gain continues with more vigor in the coming years, Lao PDR should have a system in place that productively utilizes revenues to benefit its people while being accountable and meeting international norms.

NT2 Hydropower Facility and Related Infrastructure

Soon after ground was broken in November 2005, construction activities went into full gear. At the peak of construction, the project employed nearly 10,000 workers, 80 percent of them Lao. NTPC and its contractors were able to mobilize the best personnel from the international market to build the state-of-the-art dam and associated infrastructure, which included measures to minimize environmental and social impacts. Along the way, foreign experts were able to transfer know-how to thousands of skilled and unskilled local laborers involved in the project. Initially, the company had to hire more than the anticipated number of Lao laborers because of competency gaps and low productivity. Productivity improved as construction completion approached. The Lao mechanics, fitters, electricians, carpenters, and masons who worked on the project have found jobs in other construction projects, including hydropower, mining, and road building—an early indication of NT2's potential to build capacity at all levels through its operating life.

The construction met with its share of hitches and unanticipated events, however, which have been (and in some cases are being) dealt with to achieve the necessary outcomes. For example, tunneling through 600 meters of limestone formation along the downstream channel proved to be a technological challenge. Because conventional methods could have caused a costly cave-in, the project employed a more expensive technology to accomplish the job. The road works had numerous engineering and design flaws that required corrective action by the contractor. The process of assembling and testing the turbines experienced teething problems, which have been addressed.

The physical transformation on the Nakai plateau is remarkable. The fact that the complex infrastructure and power facility have been completed almost on time and budget is a tribute to the many engineers, planners, mechanics, geologists, and others who worked on the project. The project achieved commercial operations in April 2010 with a 4-month delay and a relatively small cost overrun of about $40 million (over base cost, remaining within expected contingencies)—small numbers for a project construction period of 54 months and a base cost estimate of $1.25 billion.

The private sector, particularly Electricité de France (EdF), has played a vital role in NT2. EdF's dual role as the major shareholder of NTPC and the head contractor has been scrutinized from a variety of angles, by other shareholders, lenders, the government, and independent monitoring agencies. EdF was eager to embellish its reputation as a responsible power company capable of building hydropower plants that stand up to the greatest scrutiny and rigor. This commitment drove EdF's management to deploy solid and competent professionals to lead the two arms of their operations. To date, the potential for conflicts of interest has been managed satisfactorily through separate reporting lines within the EdF organization (EdF International holds EdF's shares in NTPC). When situations such as inadequate attention to environmental impacts of construction (excessive vegetation clearance in road widening, management of wastewater from worker camps, monitoring of sediment flow, handling of waste disposal, mitigation of road dust, and so forth) or poor quality of works by subcontractors arose, independent monitoring entities or the international financial institutions raised the issues, which were addressed by senior levels of EdF management, to ensure satisfactory resolution.

The Environmental and Social Programs

Implementation of the programs addressing social and environmental impacts, which requires achieving behavioral and mindset changes, was always expected to require a longer timeline, be more difficult, and carry greater risk than the infrastructure and electro-mechanical works. Both the government and NTPC had limited experience in undertaking such a complex operation. In view of this, the concession agreement delineated the responsibilities for implementing the environmental and social programs as shared by NTPC and the government and defined their respective obligations. NTPC has full responsibility for mitigating construction-related impacts and compensating land taking. The government is fully responsible for protecting and managing the watershed. The resettlement program has been co-implemented by both parties, with NTPC responsible for meeting the target of doubling household income by the beginning of the fifth year after relocation. The downstream program is also being co-implemented by both parties, with a cap placed on financing by NTPC, beyond which costs are the government's responsibility.

The environmental and social programs experienced a slow start. Staffing needs were underestimated at the planning stage and required twice as many persons, and the hiring of professionals took much longer than planned. The presence of experienced international experts helped bring knowledge and tested approaches from other countries; national staff had good understanding of the local situation. The combination of international and national staff proved to be an asset in implementing the different components of the program. At the same time, forging a single organizational ethos presented a challenge to NTPC. It took nearly two years and two rounds of management changes for a stable structure to emerge, which is now fully geared to deliver results.

Although the project's financial closure took place in June 2005, physical activities relating to resettlement of the 6,200 affected people on the Nakai plateau could commence only in November 2005, after the wet season. NTPC and the district teams used the intervening time to continue their consultations with the affected villages to firm up relocation plans, including plot clearance approach and house design preferences, and to start skills training in livelihood activities. The consultation and planning took more time than expected. With the help of the district teams, the villagers decided not to wait any longer and began clearing their plots. By mid-2006, half of the affected villagers had moved their homes and belongings to their new plots with help from the project, while the construction of new houses and community facilities was still ongoing.

The proactive efforts of the villagers could be attributed to the extensive local consultations with NT2–affected villagers, which have been undertaken on the project for years, empowering the villagers. These efforts have made the villagers aware of their rights and what is due to them. Not only local villagers but also district and provincial officials realized the importance and benefits of having community inputs in designing, implementing, and adapting interventions in which villagers are the eventual beneficiaries. After years of consultations and expectations, resettlers are enjoying proper houses, running water, and functioning schools and dispensaries, and the project's health program has achieved measurable improvements (based on district statistics collected over the past four years) in the well-being of the resettlers. The ongoing consultation process continues to empower villagers. It is embedded as an important modality in working with communities to identify their preferred solutions, whether these solutions are in locating school buildings or developing an organizational structure for running the village forest association.

Building empowerment among villagers is a noteworthy achievement of the project given the single-party political structure and tight centralized planning. The NT2 resettlement process serves as a model for other hydropower projects under consideration or construction. The government has facilitated site visits to NT2 for many affected communities of other projects, responding to villager requests to see and learn from the Nakai experience.

As the implementation timeline marched on, various activities ran into challenges that took time to resolve. For example, NTPC and the international financial institutions disagreed on the unit of analysis for implementation of the program outlined in the Social Development Plan (2004). NTPC preferred a thematic modular approach (providing housing to all villages as one turnkey piece, for example), whereas the international financial institutions argued for implementing the program on a village-by-village basis. The final approach adopted was a combination of both, but it took more time than envisioned to reach agreement.

Shortages in timber for resettler housing also caused delays. As the deadline for sealing the diversion channel (which would initiate the process of reservoir filling) was approaching, NTPC and the Resettlement Management Committee had to dramatically step up the pace of activities. By April 2008, all affected villages had been relocated to their new sites, within the chosen spiritual boundaries, complete with roads, electricity, water and sanitation, schools, and dispensaries. The physical resettlement program ended up costing more than the original budget.

Concurrently with the resettlement process, NTPC, the Resettlement Management Committee, and the districts began the task of developing the livelihoods of resettlers, many of whom were once hunter gatherers, accustomed to practicing "slash and burn" agriculture. This goal was always considered difficult, because it would entail adaptation by resettlers to a new way of living. Poor soil quality on the plateau where resettlers chose to move hampered rice cultivation, compounding the problem. Through extensive surveys, consultations, technical reviews, experimentation and demonstrations, and discussions involving NTPC, district officials, the international financial institutions, and the Environmental and Social Panel of Experts, a multi-pronged approach is being adapted by resettlers to overcome concerns about achieving sufficient outputs from the land.

The forestry pillar of the livelihood program also saw initial teething problems in the establishment of the village forestry association, a community-based business organization to manage community forestry activities. The process of communities taking real ownership of the association (the land and the business) will take many years; significant challenges remain in sustaining the village forestry association as a viable business model. Villagers earned their first dividends from its operations in mid-2009. The livestock pillar endured its share of difficulties, including excessive numbers of buffalos for the carrying capacity of the land and shrinking fodder space because of the reservoir formation. Through a process involving villagers, NTPC and the district determined the optimum number of buffalo and put in place programs to sell the rest. In the initial period following resettlement, the fisheries pillar emerged as an income booster for villagers, who enjoyed a fishing bonanza from the newly formed reservoir. (The large windfall is recognized as temporary;

over time, fish populations in the reservoir are expected to adjust toward a more normal equilibrium.) The functioning of the fisheries association is still in its early stages; cross-learning from the village forestry association experience is providing useful guidance.

The NTPC has been measuring household income since 2006 to gauge progress toward meeting the target of doubling household income among resettled villagers, the key indicator for the resettlement process. The project has been collecting household data on a monthly basis, conducting more detailed Living Standards Measurement Study site surveys once or twice a year.

In the short term, swings in income patterns have been noticed as a result of off-farm labor, fishing windfall, forestry dividends, and agriculture experimentation, among other factors. In addition to their contribution to the long-term targets, these measurements have also given NTPC and district officials' insights about income patterns. The first outcome milestone will be in 2012; as this date draws closer, it is only natural to expect data collection and analytical (income versus consumption) and statistical methods to come under greater scrutiny.

Adaptive management, extensive community consultations, coordinated work of NTPC and the government, and timely deployment of technical expertise have significantly helped shape the livelihood program during implementation. Looking ahead, the government will need to continue to enhance the capacity of its agencies as well as that of communities, so that a gradual approach can be taken to deliver the range of activities designed to support the resettled villagers and help ensure that resettler rights to resources and benefits are protected from outsiders wanting a share of the benefits.

The protection of the 4,000-square-kilometer NT2 watershed got off to a promising start with the establishment and staffing of the Watershed Management and Protection Authority (WMPA). The WMPA was supported by $6.5 million in funding from the project during the construction period; it receives $1 million annually (indexed to inflation) over the 25-year post-construction concession period. The funding pays for staff salaries, facilities and equipment, international and national consultants, and specialized tasks, such as biodiversity assessments wildlife monitoring, patrolling and enforcement, and land use planning.

It is too early to determine whether WMPA has been effective. Directionally, the organization is approaching its goals of balancing conservation and development in the appropriate way, but the challenges of protecting such a vast and rich area cannot be underestimated. On a positive note, reemergence of habitats and sightings of some species after many years of absence suggest that efforts have been effective and provide promising opportunities to continue and enhance conservation. On the negative side, rosewood poaching, mining activities in adjacent areas, and detection of wildlife snares are indicative of the challenges ahead. The formation of the reservoir has made access to the protected area easier, compounding the challenges. Going forward, to facilitate long-term success in protection efforts, high priority should continue to be given to maintaining an enhanced authorizing environment; ensuring autonomy of the WMPA; cultivating a close working relationship between the province and the WMPA; enhancing monitoring and patrolling measures; implementing effective measures to prosecute those engaging in poaching, logging, and mining activities; strengthening efforts to support livelihood activities for the 5,800 people living in the enclave villages; and achieving better management of watershed access from the reservoir. Long-term protection of the NT2 watershed will continue to require the high-level political support of the government on a continuing basis.

The wildlife program managed by the NTPC involving different conservation groups and experts has made important achievements, particularly in the areas of elephant management and wildlife rescue. After surveying the elephant population, the Wildlife Conservation Society created eight mineral licks in the watershed for the 140–150 elephants living in the plateau, an effort that is helping in their move to the watershed. The Society is also training government counterparts to help villagers protect crops from elephants by using alarm/barrier fences and noise making. As the reservoir filled in 2008, the wildlife rescue team rescued 264 animals, which it released to the watershed. The rescue and release into the wild of the 37 large-antlered muntjacs (an endangered species endemic to the Annamites) is a noteworthy success. In addition, 490 turtles and tortoises from 7 species were captured from areas to be inundated and relocated to suitable habitats and reconstructed wetlands. There is more work to be done by both the government and NTPC before sustainability can be ensured, but the wildlife program serves as a benchmark for other hydropower projects to replicate.

Before the formation of the reservoir in 2008, the government undertook salvage logging and biomass clearance activities in areas that were to be permanently inundated. Salvage logging was largely completed in the summer of 2008, when less than the anticipated amount of commercially valuable timber was harvested. In June 2009, the government restarted salvage logging of areas that will be permanently inundated below the (reservoir full supply) level of 538 meters above sea level. It temporarily suspended activities until further review because of concerns expressed by the international financial institutions and the Environmental and Social Panel of Experts on the threats this will pose to the NT2 watershed (which is adjacent to the reservoir). Biomass clearance of vegetation that was left after salvage logging was not precisely agreed upfront during project design—and there were technical arguments for and against it.

A large portion of the permanent "dead zone" of 80 square kilometers (the area that would always remain under the water of the reservoir) was cleared just before the diversion channel was closed in April 2008. The additional clearance did contribute to the improvement of the water quality in the reservoir, especially near the villages, as well as navigation, and there were fewer reported fish kills compared with similar situations elsewhere. More broadly, the salvage logging operation serves as a model for similar operations planned in other future hydropower sites.

The speed of construction activities in project lands—downstream channel, roads, power lines, and others—and the social impacts of land acquisition moved more quickly than anticipated at the design stage. NTPC found it necessary to step up efforts—including by hiring additional workers and improving data management—to resolve the issues. The grievance mechanism (which NT2 pioneered in the Lao context for use in the project lands and other project areas) was also streamlined. As a result, many affected people sought redress for unfair determination of compensation. Originally, land-for-land compensation was planned involving a top-down approach, under which NTPC and the government would identify vacant land and give it as compensation to villagers who lost land. However, the lack of land in close proximity to the land lost prompted the affected people to seek cash compensation, which they used to buy land elsewhere or invest in livelihood activities. NTPC facilitated such land transactions and extended technical assistance to the affected people to start businesses such as mushroom cultivation, pig raising, fish ponds, and horticulture, among others.

During the late stages of project design (2003–05), extensive discussion took place between NTPC and the international financial institutions on the range of impacts in the downstream areas of the Nam Theun and Xe Bang Fai rivers. This debate was also the subject of considerable scrutiny by the international community. NTPC contended that the state-of-the-art engineering measures of the project would reduce environmental impacts in the two downstream areas and preferred a wait-and-see contingent approach to addressing any impacts. Based on the studies conducted and experience gained elsewhere, the international financial institutions and the Environmental and Social Panel of Experts were convinced that there would be impacts, noting that the only unknown factor was their scale and range. In the end, NTPC agreed to finance and co-implement (with the government) a downstream program in both areas. The aim of the $16 million downstream program was to proactively cushion the impacts, if and when they occurred, on the 70,000 people living along the mainstream Xe Bang Fai River and tributaries, through a combination of mitigation, compensation, and development efforts. Collectively, these efforts are already contributing to livelihoods and welfare. The development benefits are likely to extend to a larger population of people living along the two rivers.

After a slow start in the form of a pilot approach, the program has now been scaled up to cover all affected mainstream villages. The most important aspect of the downstream program has been the active participation of the villages, district working groups, and the company to collectively implement village-level plans, whether they involve installing flood gates, compensating individual losses of river bank gardens, or implementing the successful savings and credit scheme (in which 40 percent of the poorest villagers are participating). Critics and some independent monitors remain doubtful about the adequacy of the $16 million funding for the program. Whether more funding is needed can be determined definitively only once the nature and scope of impacts become evident. Any additional funding needs beyond 2014 would need to be financed by the government, possibly using part of the NT2 revenues, which it has indicated it is willing to do based on the merits of the case. Such a situation should be approached carefully to avoid any emergence of a dependency syndrome among the downstream population.

Implementing the project's environmental and social programs has proved to be as challenging as anticipated at the time of design. These programs will continue for a long time, some possibly throughout the life of the concession period. The first five years of implementation provided a strong foundation for future efforts. The government and NTPC have approached the project thus far with a "no stone left unturned" mindset.

Despite the project's impressive performance to date, many questions remain. Will the 6,200 affected people on the Nakai plateau achieve their household and village-level income targets within the agreed timeframe, or will they be project dependent for a generation to come? Will the conservation integrity of the NT2 watershed remain intact despite the pressures from logging, mining, and wildlife trading interests from inside and outside the country? The answers to these and other questions will depend in large part on how implementation goes in the coming years.

The Lao government has lived up to its commitments, intervening at all levels to resolve problems as they arose. In the process, the government has acquired significant capacity to implement such programs. This is the single most important outcome at this point. Beginning with a handful of trained personnel, the project has trained several hundred Lao environmental and social professionals through its learning-by-doing approach. These professionals, and others now studying in new programs started by the Lao National University, will form the backbone of Lao PDR's expanding hydropower industry in the coming decades as it implements the 2005 National Policy on Environmental and Social Sustainability of the Hydropower Sector. Taking advantage of lessons learned from NT2, the government is redrafting its overall approach to environmental and social impact assessment and monitoring, with a new agency and decree expected to be in place shortly, supported by the World Bank's Lao Environment and Social Project. NTPC should also be credited for its steadfast commitment to ensuring that the environmental and social obligations are fully met. Temptations to declare early victory and reduce efforts should be avoided by continuing this commitment. For the World Bank, other international financial institutions, and the international community as a whole, NT2 will remain on the radar as a high-risk, high-reward project as implementation continues through the operations phase.

International Support

The NT2 project attracted considerable international attention in the period leading up to World Bank approval in March 2005. The government and NTPC committed to independent monitoring of the project and ensured an open and transparent process through which they would share information with the numerous stakeholders. That commitment continues to be met.

The project monitoring structure put in place during the preparation stage was enhanced during implementation in response to the demands of the international community. In addition to the Environmental and Social Panel of Experts and the International Advisory Group, a number of other entities were established. These included the independent monitoring agencies for the watershed, downstream, plateau resettlement, and project lands; the lenders' engineer/technical advisor; and the independent government engineer. In practice, this combination created a very complex and layered approach that placed heavy burdens on the government and NTPC staff. The various entities were all mandated by some legal agreement for the project and were subject to rigorous supervision and monitoring by the international financial institutions. Simplification of this system would have meant time-consuming exercises involving amendments to legal agreements. Instead, a conscientious effort was made to streamline the monitoring schedules and reduce the overlaps between the entities while not diminishing overall effectiveness. The Environmental and Social Panel of Experts and the lenders' technical adviser had near regulatory authority on the project. The Panel, though advisory to the government, had certain responsibilities under the concession agreement to make determinations on prior actions before certain project milestones; it had to strike a delicate balance between providing constructive guidance and respecting sovereignty sensitivities. Effective intervention by the Panel, through their 13th and 14th visits (between January and April 2008) ensured that the physical resettlement program on the Nakai plateau not only was expedited but also met the obligations of the concession agreement before the start of reservoir filling (marked by closure of the diversion tunnel in mid-April 2008). The fact that the Panel enjoyed the confidence of senior government leaders greatly helped in resolving matters. The lenders' technical adviser has a mandatory role to play under the project's financing agreement; its quarterly visits have been the most frequent of those by all independent monitoring entities. It established grounds for compliance versus noncompliance, at the same time providing technical assistance to NTPC. Based on the experience thus far, there is considerable scope to simplify the monitoring arrangements as the operating context changes beyond the commercial operation date.

NTPC has supported knowledge exchange, transparency, and disclosure in a number of ways. It has gone beyond requirements, making available a number of operational documents and technical studies through its Web site; encouraging visits by media and civil society groups to the project site, facilitating unhindered access to the project site and affected villages; organizing annual stakeholder workshops that provide information on the status of the project work; and supporting peer-to-peer learning among hydropower projects (for example, hydropower operators of new projects in

Lao PDR, Tajikistan, Thailand, and Vietnam). The annual stakeholder forum
has provided a platform for meaningful two-way dialogue. However, it has
grown from about 60 participants in the first year to more than 300 participants in 2008, diminishing its usefulness. This circumstance has prompted
the government and NTPC to rethink the way this forum should be organized. Media interest in the project remains strong—with several feature pieces
written in a variety of electronic and print media outlets worldwide, covering
a range of topics including discussion of the project's pros and cons, challenges
faced by the people, threats to the biodiversity of the area, country political
issues, and performance of the international financial institutions—and interest in the project is expected to continue for years to come. Meaningful sharing of information will remain an important effort.

Peer-to-peer learning opportunities, including the Hydropower High Level
Forum between Lao PDR and Thailand in September 2007, have proven to
be extremely useful in knowledge sharing. This forum brought together, for
the first time, government representatives of the two countries, private sector
developers, financing institutions, international financial institutions, and
civil society to discuss the emerging NT2 practices and how they could be
replicated. The forum ended with a communiqué for furthering such practices
in future hydropower investments. Following this, the Mekong River Commission launched a consultative exercise in which developers of potential
mainstream dams shared information with one another, increasing their collective understanding of the cumulative impacts that will affect the river's
ecosystem and the livelihoods it supports.

Collaboration and cooperation with the international financial institutions
during implementation has been remarkably good and constructive, facilitating coordination across a large number of institutions. This was achieved
through two half-yearly technical missions, one of which also served as an annual management mission, and through fortnightly audio conferences during
the first 18 months. In addition, the World Bank, the Asian Development
Bank, and Agence Française de Développement strengthened their field presence significantly with a variety of technical specialists who provided real
time advice to NTPC and ensured that the fiduciary issues were well handled.
The teams worked seamlessly, with considerable knowledge sharing among
the staff of the institutions.

International support was also catalyzed in the form of enhanced donor
funding to implement Lao PDR's Sixth National Socio-Economic Development Plan (2006–10). At the roundtable meeting held in November 2006,

the country's development partners pledged nearly $400 million annually to finance the implementation of the Five-Year Plan. At the same meeting, the government and 22 development partners signed the Vientiane Declaration on Aid Effectiveness to advance the Paris Agenda. Since then, the World Bank has been leading several multidonor efforts to support the implementation of government reforms—namely, budget support operations (the Poverty Reduction Support Operation series), trust funds for trade and public finance management, and the education sectorwide initiative.

The government has largely lived up to the expectations of the international community on the commitments it made on the NT2 project, strengthening trust over the years. The country is beginning to see dividends from its engagement with the international community through NT2 in the form of investments, trade, aid, and knowledge.

The NT2 project has already helped transform Lao PDR through new institutions and policies, setting a sound foundation for springing forward to become a middle-income country by 2020. NT2 appears to be poised to achieve sustainable outcomes over the long term. It is tempting to try to draw final conclusions, but the process is still unfolding. Challenges will continue to arise, and experiences will continue to inform future decisions and efforts. The more complete body of experiences and lessons available down the road will enrich a deeper analysis and assessment, which should be documented and shared at an opportune point in the future.

Index

V

Vientiane Declaration on Aid
Effectiveness, 175
Vietic (ethnic group), 56
Vietnam
   bilateral agreement with, 7
   business forums in, 161
   consultations in, 101
   electricity demand in, 158
   foreign direct investment from, 38
   Greater Mekong subregion and, 32n4
   Lao PDR border with, 5
   Mekong River Commission and,
      31n2
   Nam Theun watershed and, 57
   peer-to-peer learning from, 163
   wildlife and logging agreement with,
      65
village facilitators for consultations, 102,
   142
vulnerable groups. See indigenous peoples;
   minorities

W

"wait and see" approach to downstream
   risks, 66, 170–171
water quality
   reducing impacts to, 60
   in reservoir, 170
   in Xe Bang Fai basin, 58–59
Water Resources and Environment
   agency, 158
Water Resources Sector Strategy, 11
Watershed Management and Protection
   Authority (WMPA), 30, 65, 152,
   168–169
waterways, international, 54b
WCD (World Commission on Dams), 1,
   11, 101
Web sites
   for communications, 120, 142, 153
   for project management, 108
   for transparency, 31, 111, 173
   for workshops, 114
Wildlife Conservation Society, 10, 169
wildlife management, 30, 169
wildlife surveys, 66

WMPA (Watershed Management and
   Protection Authority), 30, 65, 152,
   168–169
women in resettlement process, 57b
workshops, international, 13, 24,
   112–114, 142
World Bank
   ADB and AFD partnership with, 86
   alternative supply sources, 74–76
   capacity-building strategies of, 46,
      69, 94–96, 162
   communications strategy, 24–25, 70,
      117–125
   concession agreement, 87
   consensus building by, 41–44
   consultations and, 80–81, 101–102
   CPIA scores of, 50n1
   criticisms of, 20, 127–128
   downstream risks assessments, 66
   due diligence of, 42, 49–50, 86, 138
   EIRR analysis, 79
   electricity demand forecasting, 73–74
   environmental and social safeguards,
      1, 52, 76, 86, 87–89, 98n5, 128,
      134–136
   expertise of, 80, 174
   financial partners' perceptions, 85–90
   financiers, mobilization of, 82–83
   government track record assessment
      and, 45–46
   lessons learned, 25–27, 90–96,
      127–145
   management framework under, 39,
      40–41, 48–50
   mitigation planning by, 67
   as multilateral funder, 116n1
   poverty reduction strategy, 36–38,
      44–45
   project boundaries, defining, 61–63
   project preparation strategy, 17–22,
      33–35, 48–50, 51, 93–94
   replicability of project, 96–97
   stakeholders and, 9–16, 23–24,
      105–116
   Structural Adjustment Credit from,
      35–36
   sustainability assessments, 77–78